WHISPERS FROM

Heaven

for the Christmas Spirit

Illustrated by Michael Jaroszko

Publications International, Ltd.

Contents

❦ ❦ ❦

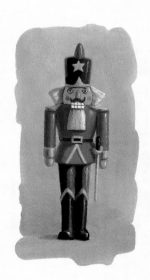

Capturing the Christmas Spirit

IN A BUSTLING CAFÉ just before Christmas, a two-year-old boy sips hot chocolate with his family. The child can't hear the chatter and laughter, because he is deaf, but he does notice the kind smile of a young man seated near the door. Adept in sign language, the man forms the signs for "How are you?" and "You are beautiful." The boy's blue eyes sparkle as he turns to his mom, who is deeply touched by the man's small but kind gesture toward her son. "There aren't many moments like that for him," Susan Fahncke writes, "and I will treasure the memory always." "You Are Beautiful" is one of the dozens of stories in this book that capture the spirit of Christmas.

The story of Jesus' birth overflows with strong emotions: wonder, anticipation, anxiety, love, joy.... And those who visited the newborn king were overwhelmed by the glorious presence of the Lord. Thus, it seems fitting that we experience similar feelings each year as Christmas Day approaches.

Children toss excitedly in their beds on Christmas Eve, wondering what their magical Santa will bring. Adults immersed in the festivities of the season often pause momentarily, overcome by their love for family, friends, and the Lord. Conversely, for the lonely and destitute, Christmas can be the worst time of the year. Good or bad, Christmas is a season of powerful emotions.

In Chapter 2 of this book, "The Spirit of Giving," Elaine Slater Reese tells the poignant story of a furnace repairman, working at a customer's home during the Christmas season. Dressed in grimy work clothes, his expression revealing years of suffering, the man seems painfully out of place in the Christmasy Wisconsin house. He stares sadly and states, "We don't celebrate Christmas at our house no more." The man explains how his son was killed in an auto accident and how he and his wife—now crippled—live in a near-empty apartment, enduring the daily pain of their loss. The homeowner, deeply moved, offers the man a special gift. "Lady," he says, "there ain't never been nobody cared about my wife and me. There ain't nobody ever gave us nothing." Then he smiles. "Now I can give my wife a present for Christmas."

This book brims with inspirational stories of giving, love, spirit, and cheer. "A Slice of Life" tells the tale of orphans who receive tangy, sweet oranges for Christmas—except for one brokenhearted lad who's left empty-handed. However, when his pals see how dejected he is, they decide to give him one segment each—enough to piece together a full orange.

Stories in the concluding chapter, "Holiday Cheer," offer up smiles and laughs. The sisters in "Reindeer on the Roof" recall the time when Dad climbed the roof and pretended to be Santa coming in for a landing. Unfortunately, he was overcome by his fear of heights, prompting the arrival of a police car and a fire truck, not to mention a TV news crew.

Perhaps you've become jaded by Christmas as you've gotten older, or maybe you sometimes get overwhelmed by the shopping, wrapping, and busywork that accompany the holiday. Take a moment to read from the pages of *Whispers from Heaven for the Christmas Spirit.* The stories will warm your heart and encourage your own Christmas spirit.

The Magic of the Season

HE SPRANG IN HIS SLEIGH, to his team gave a whistle,
And away they all flew like the down of a thistle;
But I heard him exclaim, ere he drove out of sight;
"Happy Christmas to all, and to all a good-night!"

CLEMENT C. MOORE (1779–1863)
"A VISIT FROM ST. NICHOLAS"

Ansel's Special Gift

A NSEL NORDQUIST STEADIED HIMSELF against the cold night wind. Tightly gripping his gold-knobbed cane, he stared at the bright and lovely things in the Saks Fifth Avenue window. "What to get?" he asked himself. He needed to buy only one present, but it had to be perfect. Perfect. Just right. And time was running out.

Snowflakes, thick and fluffy, tumbled through the air. In the street beside him, a dapple-gray horse with steaming breath pulled a carriage of young lovers beneath the stars and twinkling Christmas lights.

Busy shoppers scurried by, feet crunching in the new-fallen snow. Faintly, he heard the *ting . . . ting . . . ting* of The Salvation Army bell. The air was heavy with freshly cut pine mixed with the smell of hot popcorn from the street vendor's cart.

A gleeful toddler squealed, "Hurry, Mommy! Come on! Come on!" He tugged hard at his mother's skirt, pulling her from the boring windows filled with gowns and jewels and furs to the exciting windows, down the street, loaded with wondrous toys.

Ansel turned cautiously, steadied by his cane, and shuffled toward the next Saks window, wondering what beautiful things it would hold. His cashmere coat and white silk scarf kept him warm against the chill. Nevertheless, the bitter wind brought tears to his eyes. Or was it the wind? Perhaps, instead, it was the season.

Window after window, Ansel passed. Each was filled with different things that, at various times in his life, he had bought. The diamond ring. The wedding band. The casual and the elegant clothes. The maternity wear and the baby things. The toys. Oh, yes, the toys. Especially the ones that came in pieces and had to be assembled.

How she'd laugh and how he'd curse, trying to put the toys together. She'd bring him coffee. They'd sit and talk of Christmases past. She'd drink the milk and eat the cookies the children had left for Santa. Then, when all the work was done, they'd sit on the floor in front of the fire and pray to the child who had changed the world. They'd pray to the Prince of Peace. They'd kiss. They'd hold each other close. They'd feel the fear of all the world and the safety of each other. Yes, these were the times when they knew love best. These were the fullest of years.

A smile crept across Ansel's face. *"Wonderful, wonderful times,"* he thought. *"But my gift . . . I must find my gift."*

Ansel turned from Saks and walked down the street. Past the haberdashery. Past the bakery. Past the laughter-filled café. He came to a stop at the toy store window. He watched the circling electric train running through mountains and villages. The sailboats. Airplanes with gas engines. Mesmerized, he watched them all, losing himself in the ghosts of the past and their hollow, faraway laughter.

Then a shiver ran down his spine. Despite his hat and gloves and coat, Ansel was growing cold. He was growing tired. But nothing . . . nothing could he find. He could not find his treasured gift.

Then he saw it! There it was! Tucked in the corner. High on a shelf. Up behind the expensive toys. Yes! There it was. The perfect gift. The most perfect gift of all.

Ansel entered the shop and purchased the gift, requesting that it be nicely wrapped. Then he walked back to the street and hailed a cab.

"Where to?" the cabby asked.

"St. Elizabeth's Hospital," Ansel replied.

Upon arriving at the hospital, Ansel paid the driver, tipping him nicely. Each wished the other a Merry Christmas. Ansel shuffled through the lobby to the elevator, taking it to the fourth floor—to Sarah's room.

Once inside, Ansel removed his hat, gloves, and coat. He pulled the chair close to Sarah. He took her hand and gently stroked it.

"Hello, Sarah," he said, not expecting an answer. . . . None came.

Ansel gazed at her beauty. The rest of the world saw her 80-year-old wrinkles, frail white hair, and swollen, gnarled, arthritic joints. But not Ansel. Oh, with his eyes he saw those things, but not with his heart.

What Ansel saw was a woman who had devoted her life to him. She was a young woman high on a ladder, giggling, with paint in her hair. A woman on the sidewalk in front of their house playing hopscotch with the neighborhood kids. A woman with skin like farm-fresh cream—ripe, round, and aglow with child.

His heart heard her soft lullabies rocking their children to sleep. It heard her laughter as she ran with them on the lawn, jumping into piles of bright autumn leaves.

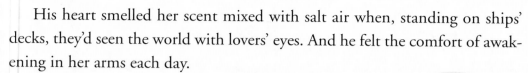

His heart smelled her scent mixed with salt air when, standing on ships' decks, they'd seen the world with lovers' eyes. And he felt the comfort of awakening in her arms each day.

Yes. This was the Sarah that Ansel's heart saw. Not the Sarah connected to life by various wires and tubes.

"It's Christmas Eve, Sarah," Ansel said softly. "I brought you a gift. Would you like to open it now or save it for tomorrow?"

Knowing that Sarah couldn't answer, Ansel reached for the gift and placed it on the bed beside her. "OK. We'll open it now. See the beautiful ribbon, Sarah? And the paper? Red. Your favorite. I picked it out especially for you. And I watched to make sure they wrapped it right. Just for you."

With aged, trembling fingers, Ansel unwrapped the gift. While doing so, he journeyed back through time. . . .

"The cow's gone dry, Ma!" Ansel hollered, walking through the door.

"What'll we do, Pa?" Sarah yelled back, busy in the kitchen.

"Shoot her an' have her for dinner, I guess."

"OK, Pa. Best git out an' shoot her."

This was their greeting each night when Ansel came home from work. How it began, they couldn't remember. Just silliness. Just being young. It certainly had nothing to do with them. They didn't live on a farm. They lived in the city. And Ansel couldn't milk a cow. He was an attorney. All they knew was that it was fun. It was theirs and no one else's. It was their special way of saying, "I love you. Good to be home."

Ansel pulled the last of the wrapping from the box. "Here it is, Sarah. It's all unwrapped. Here . . . give me your hands." Ansel drew her hands toward him so that Sarah could hold the gift. Then he placed it in her palms. It was a small, fuzzy stuffed toy—a brown and white cow that mooed when squeezed. The cow lay in Sarah's limp hands. Ansel reached and squeezed the cow. "Moo...moo..."

In the silence, Ansel heard a sound—quiet, soft, muffled. Looking from the toy to her face, he saw Sarah's eyes—open, distant, glassy. Her lips moved slightly. Ansel rose from his chair, standing in disbelief. Months—months it had been—since Sarah had stirred.

Gently, afraid of breaking the spell, Ansel leaned toward Sarah, turning his ear to her lips. "What, my dear? What did you say?"

Quiet as wind-driven snow, Sarah whispered, "What'll we do, Pa?"

Never had Ansel felt such joy! These few words from Sarah's lips! What a gift! What a gift! Never had there been such a wonderful gift! Tears welled in Ansel's eyes, falling on Sarah's cheek. *Our words! Our special words!* he thought, then chokingly replied, "Shoot her an' have her for dinner, I guess."

Into the night, this holy night, Ansel waited for Sarah's response. . . .

But Sarah lay silent. She held her cow. She sailed into the great beyond. . . .

BY LARRY E. SCOTT

❧　　❧　　❧　　❧

For to us a child is born, to us a son is given; and the government will be upon his shoulder, and his name will be called "Wonderful Counselor, Mighty God, Everlasting Father, Prince of Peace."

ISAIAH 9:6

A Slice of Life

❦ ❦ ❦

*J*EAN HEAVED ANOTHER world-weary sigh. Tucking a strand of shiny black hair behind her ear, she frowned at the teetering tower of Christmas cards waiting to be signed. What was the point? How could she sign only one name? A "couple" required two people, and she was just one.

The legal separation from Don had left her feeling vacant and incomplete. Maybe she would skip the cards this year. And the holiday decorating. Truthfully, even a tree felt like more than she could manage. She had canceled out of the caroling party and the church nativity pageant. Christmas was to be shared, and she had no one to share it with.

The doorbell's insistent ring startled her. Padding to the door in her thick socks, Jean cracked it open against the frigid December night. She peered into the empty darkness of the porch. Instead of a friendly face—something she could use about now—she found only a jaunty green gift bag perched on the railing. *From whom?* she wondered. *And why?*

Under the bright kitchen light, she pulled out handfuls of shredded gold tinsel, feeling for a gift. Instead, her fingers plucked an envelope from the bottom. Tucked inside was a typed letter. It was a . . . story?

The little boy was new to the Denmark orphanage, and Christmas was drawing near, Jean read. Already caught up in the tale, she settled into a kitchen chair.

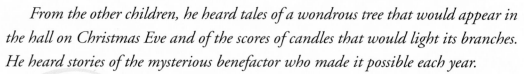

From the other children, he heard tales of a wondrous tree that would appear in the hall on Christmas Eve and of the scores of candles that would light its branches. He heard stories of the mysterious benefactor who made it possible each year.

The little boy's eyes opened wide at the mere thought of all that splendor. The only Christmas tree he had ever seen was through the fogged windows of other people's homes. There was even more, the children insisted. More? Oh, yes! Instead of the orphanage's regular fare of gruel, they would be served fragrant stew and crusty, hot bread that special night.

Last, and best of all, the little boy learned, each of them would receive a holiday treat. He would join the line of children to get his very own. . . .

Jean turned the page. Instead of a continuation, she was startled to read: "Everyone needs to celebrate Christmas, wouldn't you agree? Watch for Part II." She refolded the paper while a faint smile teased the corner of her mouth.

The next day was so busy that Jean forgot all about the story. That evening, she rushed home from work. If she hurried, she'd probably have enough time to decorate the mantle. She pulled out the box of garland, only to drop it when the doorbell rang. Opening the door, she found herself looking at a red gift bag. She reached for it eagerly and pulled out the piece of paper.

. . . to get his very own orange, Jean read. *An orange? That's a treat?* she thought incredulously.

An orange! Of his very own? Yes, the others assured him. There would be one apiece. The boy closed his eyes against the wonder of it all. A tree. Candles. A filling meal. And an orange of his very own.

He knew the smell, tangy sweet, but only the smell. He had sniffed oranges at the merchant's stall in the marketplace. Once he had even dared to rub a single fin-

ger over the brilliant, pocked skin. He fancied for days that his hand still smelled of orange. But to taste one, to eat one? Heaven.

The story ended abruptly, but Jean didn't mind. She knew more would follow.

The next evening, Jean waited anxiously for the sound of the doorbell. She wasn't disappointed. This time, though, the embossed gold bag was heavier than the others had been. She tore into the envelope resting on top of the tissue paper.

Christmas Eve was all the children had been promised. The piney scent of fir competed with the aroma of lamb stew and homey yeast bread. Scores of candles diffused the room with golden halos. The boy watched in amazement as each child in turn eagerly claimed an orange and politely said "thank you."

The line moved quickly, and he found himself in front of the towering tree and the equally imposing headmaster.

"Too bad, young man, too bad. But the count was in before you arrived. It seems there are no more oranges. Next year. Yes, next year you will receive an orange."

Brokenhearted, the orphan raced up the stairs empty-handed to bury both his face and his tears beneath his pillow.

Wait! This wasn't how she wanted the story to go. Jean felt the boy's pain, his aloneness.

The boy felt a gentle tap on his back. He tried to still his sobs. The tap became more insistent until, at last, he pulled his head from under the pillow.

He smelled it before he saw it. A cloth napkin rested on the mattress. Tucked inside was a peeled orange, tangy

THE MAGIC OF THE SEASON

sweet. It was made of segments saved from the others. A slice donated from each child. Together they added up to make one whole, complete fruit.

An orange of his very own.

Jean swiped at the tears trickling down her cheeks. From the bottom of the gift bag she pulled out an orange—a foil-covered chocolate orange—already separated into segments. And for the first time in weeks, she smiled. Really smiled.

She set about making copies of the story, wrapping individual slices of the chocolate orange. There was Mrs. Potter across the street, spending her first Christmas alone in 58 years. There was Melanie down the block, facing her second round of radiation. Her running partner, Jan, single-parenting a difficult teen. Lonely Mr. Bradford losing his eyesight, and Sue, sole care-giver to an aging mother. . . .

A piece from her might help make one whole.

BY CAROL MCADOO REHME

Christmas is so many moods and memories . . .
Christmas is the glitter of trees hung with shining
    ornaments . . .
Christmas is the glow in the eyes of a believing child.

LLEWELLYN MILLER

18 ❤ *Whispers from Heaven*

Owed to Joy

❦   ❦   ❦

THE YEAR OUR YOUNGEST daughter, Shelly, was four, she received an unusual Christmas present from "Santa."

She was the perfect age for Christmas, able to understand the true meaning of the season, but still completely enchanted by the magic of it. Her innocent joyfulness was compelling and catching—a great gift to parents, reminding us of what Christmas should represent no matter how old we are.

The most highly prized gift Shelly received that Christmas Eve was a giant bubble-maker, a simple device of plastic and cloth the inventor promised would create huge billowing bubbles, large enough to swallow a wide-eyed four-year-old. Both Shelly and I were excited about trying it out, but it was after dark so we'd have to wait until the next day.

Later that night I read the instruction booklet while Shelly played with some of her other new toys. The inventor of the bubble-maker had tried all types of soaps for formulating bubbles and found that Joy dishwashing detergent created the best giant bubbles. I'd have to buy some.

The next morning, I was awakened very early by small stirrings in the house. Shelly was up. I knew in my sleepy mind that Christmas Day festivities would soon begin, so I arose and made my way toward the kitchen to start the coffee. In the hallway, I met my daughter, already wide awake, the bubble-maker clutched in her chubby little hand, the magic of Christmas morning embraced in her four-year-old heart. Her eyes were shining with excitement, and she asked, "Daddy, can we make bubbles now?"

I sighed heavily and rubbed my eyes. I looked toward the window, where the sky was only beginning to lighten with the dawn. I looked toward the kitchen, where the coffeepot had yet to start dripping its aromatic reward for early-rising Christmas dads.

"Shelly," I said, my voice almost pleading and perhaps a little annoyed, "it's too early. I haven't even had my coffee yet."

Her smile fell away. Immediately I felt a father's remorse for bursting her bright Christmas bubble with what I suddenly realized was my own selfish problem, and my heart broke a little.

But I was a grown-up. I could fix this. In a flash of adult inspiration, I unshouldered the responsibility. Recalling the inventor's recommendation of a particular brand of bubble-making detergent—which I knew we did not have in the house—I laid the blame squarely on him, pointing out gently, "Besides, you have to have Joy."

I watched her eyes light back up as she realized, in less than an instant, that she could neutralize this small problem with the great and wonderful truth she was about to reveal.

"Oh, Daddy," she promised, with all the honesty and enthusiasm and Christmas excitement she could possibly communicate, "Oh, Daddy, I *do*."

I broke records getting to the store, and in no time at all we were out on the front lawn creating gigantic, billowing, gossamer orbs—each one filled with Joy and sent forth shimmering into the Christmas sun.

BY TED A. THOMPSON

Will Santa Come for Christmas Dinner?

❦ ❦ ❦

I FIRST SAW HIM at our friends' wedding rehearsal. The resemblance was uncanny. There was no red suit with white fur trim, no fat belly, no black boots, and no sleigh and reindeer. But the beard—the beard was the purest white I had ever seen. And naturally curly. It was the most authentic Santa beard anyone could conceive. My adult mind kept playing a childish refrain. "It's Santa! It's really Santa!"

How appropriate that the wedding would be on December 23. Santa was to provide the music. He was unusually solemn as the others celebrated in a festive mood. The minister showed him where he would stand during the ceremony. I assumed he would sing. But the thin, bearded Santa in blue jeans and a yellow sweater reached down, opened a violin case, and lovingly took out his treasured instrument.

Santa was not just a man playing a violin. It was obvious even to the untrained ear that the strings were in the hands of a master. People who had been chatting in various parts of the church slipped into the pews one by one, moved by the talent of this quiet gentleman.

To my surprise, he was seated across the table from me at the rehearsal dinner. He did look like Santa, but carrying on a conversation with him was more than a little difficult. I learned that he was a plumber, not a professional musician, and that there was no "Mrs. Claus." He would be spending Christmas alone.

He preyed on my mind all night. Santa spending Christmas alone? The next day I asked the bride-to-be, "What's with Santa? No twinkle in his eye, no family, and no one to spend Christmas with?" She looked at me. "You don't know, do you?"

I instantly knew that I was not prepared for her answer. She said that Santa loved his wife and small son very much—a devoted husband and father. Five years earlier, he came home from work in early December to find them both gone—their lives snuffed out by an intruder. He's never been the same since. The twinkle in his eyes has not returned. There is no laughter. And he can't bear to hold little children, look into their eyes, and listen to their precious requests as he had done for so many years. No more Santa in the red suit—just the plumber in blue jeans.

At the reception, he stood alone, a glass of ice-cold punch in his hand. Walking over, I managed to engage him in a couple of short sentences. "Yes, the weather was bitter cold." And, "It was a beautiful wedding." I looked him in the eye. "Santa, will you come to our house for Christmas dinner?" His face flushed. I could see his hands shaking. "We have five sons. May I tell them Santa is coming for Christmas dinner?" I slipped him a note with our address. He stared into space. I turned away unacknowledged.

As I tucked the younger boys in bed on Christmas Eve, I spoke softly. "Maybe we will have a special guest for dinner tomorrow. Who knows? Maybe Santa himself will be here!" They all giggled. "Sure, Mom. See you in the morning, Mom. Love you, Mom!" I prayed as I laid my head on the pillow. "Please don't let Santa be alone on Christmas."

The turkey was browned perfectly. The desserts were arranged on the special table, and everyone was starving. One o'clock and time for dinner. During the morning, each of the boys, one by one, had come to question me. "Mom, did you really invite him?" "Mom, do you think he's going to come?"

My answer: "I hope so, Son."

We couldn't wait any longer. "Time for Christmas dinner!" Everyone gathered around the table. I saw the disappointment in the boys' faces. Just as the "amen" at the end of the blessing was pronounced, we all heard a car door slam. The boys raced to the back door. I could tell by the amazement on their faces who was coming up the back steps. "Mom, it's him! It's him! It's really Santa Claus—in his everyday work clothes, the ones he must wear all year in his workshop!"

The boys never saw the tears I brushed away as they rushed to usher Santa in. After we opened all the presents (there were even two for Santa under the tree), Santa spoke. "May I give your family a gift now?" He went outside and came back in with his old black violin case. As he played, I was sure I could hear the angels joining in as we sang "Silent Night."

After he put the instrument away, our two-year-old toddled over to Santa and gently stroked his beard. "Santa, tan I sits on ur lap?" I saw all the color drain from Santa's cheeks. For a moment, he was as white as his beard. Then slowly, slowly, Santa eased back into his big chair, and finally he stretched out his arms.

BY ELAINE SLATER REESE

O Holy Night

❦ ❦ ❦

"So WHERE DO YOU think we will be going to church next month?" That became a common inquiry from my husband. We had moved to this mid-Atlantic hinterland and found ourselves in search of a new church. This mission was compounded by the fact that we knew no one. Weekly, we checked out a different church to find the perfect place to worship.

After months, we found the perfect place (or so we thought). It was close to home, had a great children's program, and seemed to have an appropriate amount of young, growing families. I spoke with the greeter and found out who to call. The next day, Monday, I did just that.

"Hello, may I speak with Reverend Coleman? . . . Oh, well is there a better time to reach him? My family and I have been relocated to this area, and we really like your church and your congregation and would like the appropriate paperwork to formally join."

The receptionist, who had been taking Reverend Coleman's calls, told me that we could not join the church because too many families were enrolled. A new congregation was forming, however. "Perhaps you could speak with someone there," she said. I was to call a man whom I did not know, at a place that did not exist, for a congregation that was only being formed . . . somewhere.

"Okay, we will go back to the church one more time, and maybe we can find out where this new group meets," I told my husband and children. They were agreeable, mainly because we always went to breakfast after church. The draw was not the worship but the fellowship and the feast afterward. At the next Sunday mass, the homily was actually given by the new leader of the scattered flock of people. Thus, we now had a contact; her name was Mary Lou. I called her the next day.

"Oh, yes, yes, yes!" she said. "We would love to have you join our congregation. May I stop over and introduce myself and bring the paperwork for you and your family? We are still looking for a permanent place to have our weekly church gatherings, but we are delighted that you will be joining us." Mary Lou chattered on for a while longer, and I knew we were going in the right direction, although I was not sure where.

"Mommy, I thought we were going to church," Jay questioned the following Sunday as we pulled into the parking lot of a movie theater.

"We are, sweetheart," I answered, as his daddy parked the car. Jason's eyes lit up, and he was not about to let this drop, thinking one or both of his parents had lost their minds. "Why are we here if we are supposed to be going to church?"

"The church is not a church yet, and we do not have anywhere else to go, so we are going to the movie theater," I explained. None of us really cared where we went after a few weeks, especially because on these days we began going to the movies after church, which took the place of breakfast. Pop and popcorn began to substitute for ham and eggs.

As the summer wore into autumn, and the leaves began to drop from the trees, the congregation continued to grow and the accommodations in the movie theater became too small. It was time to move on again, and the new location was, again, due to the generosity of a community member. This time we were shuffled to an old, gray barn. It was not much to look at, but it served the purpose—and our active, hard-working, and still-growing community gathered at this rustic spot, now filled with folding chairs.

It took a long time to get wiring into this dimly lit structure to supply us with light, heat, and a microphone. Reverend Appleby fortunately had a sense of humor and a booming voice. However, as October transitioned into November, and Thanksgiving ushered in Advent, our necessity for heavy coats during church became more apparent.

"Jim, make sure the kids have their gloves this morning," I said. "It is really cold. I know we should expect December weather, but the wind seems brutal today."

"Check. We have gloves and hats, and I grabbed a blanket, just in case we need it. We can wrap these little monkeys up; they'll stay warm for the hour."

The cold weather brought preparation but still no permanent church. December wore on and Christmas Eve appeared in a flash.

Again, we had the checklist before church. "Honey, let's keep the kids extra warm. It may snow tonight. Can you help me get Katie's boots on?"

Robby, our second child, mumbled, "Mommy, do we have to go? It's too cold."

"Yes, honey, we do. It is Christmas Eve, and if we have time to wait for Santa, we have time to go to church and remember Jesus' birthday."

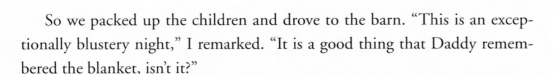

So we packed up the children and drove to the barn. "This is an exceptionally blustery night," I remarked. "It is a good thing that Daddy remembered the blanket, isn't it?"

"Yes!" the three children yelled in unison. Dusk slipped into darkness as we parked along the old country road and trudged along to the barn, children in tow, wrapped up so much that they could barely walk. We entered our familiar "church."

The old, gray barn was no longer just an old, gray barn. It had been transformed into a nativity scene—a *real* one, with a real manger and real sheep and a cow and a donkey. Hay was everywhere. The eyes of the children were filled with sheer wonder. Amid the animals were people. The woman wore a blue robe, and the man was in old, brown sackcloth tied with a rope. He held a staff, and she held an infant wrapped in swaddling clothes. They were not just people; they were the Holy Family. They were surrounded by shepherds tending the flock. I don't remember what the music was, if there was any. Nor do I remember what the homily was, if one was given. I don't even know if we stayed warm enough. I do remember being in the presence of the true spirit of Christmas. It was magnificent.

That Christmas Eve celebration could have lasted forever. We finally left the barn to find that snow was lightly falling and the stars were announcing the birth of Jesus. We all felt a silent joy at the miraculous event we had been witness to. Eventually, we did find a church to call our own. But nothing ever came close to that Christmas Eve of wonder, with Jesus in the old, gray barn.

BY ELIZABETH TOOLE

A Gift in the Trees

G OD SHOWS HIS LOVE for us in many ways. Something that may not seem extraordinary to one person might appear as a miracle for someone else. On Christmas Eve 1997, that is exactly how I saw things, though not at first. At first I was feeling too sorry for myself to see anything but my own unhappiness.

The holiday season is a popular time for couples to get engaged. I had been in three long-term relationships by the time I was 29, but none of them had ever produced a marriage proposal. I had always considered myself a loyal, caring, unselfish girlfriend, and boyfriends often told me as much *after* the relationship had ended. I always seemed to be "the one that got away," and I began to feel like I was special only once the relationship was over. After a while, I started to feel like I just wasn't worth a lifetime commitment.

At the age of 29, I decided I needed to take my own happiness into consideration. It took a couple years of dating mistakes, but I finally figured out how to respect my own needs and not just worry about the needs of my partner. That's when, at the age of 31, I met Paul. He was a wonderful person who didn't expect me to take care of him. He just wanted to be with me, and he respected me for who I was. Everything felt right between us, and I figured I had finally found a man I could marry.

During our second Christmas together, I thought Paul might propose. On December 22, we ventured onto the topic of marriage. Paul said that he did see himself marrying me, but the timing was not good "right now." I couldn't help but feel sorry for myself. So many of my friends had received proposals and engagement rings, but I had never received either. I was at the point where I figured maybe marriage just wasn't in the cards for me.

On the following day, December 23, school was canceled because of a winter storm. I knew my students would be as excited as I was for the extra day off right before the holiday break. It would also be nice to have a beautiful, white Christmas. The roads were covered in snow, and the trees were buried under a sheer layer of ice. It was much too hazardous to venture out, so I just stayed inside and reflected on my situation.

By the end of that snowy day, I had come to the conclusion that it wasn't the proposal I needed. It was simply that I wanted to feel loved and appreciated enough that someone would want to be with me forever. I prayed to God and asked that someday a man would think I was important enough to give me a diamond, the symbol of the commitment that my heart needed the most.

Christmas Eve finally arrived. Paul came to my house so we could ride together to my sister's holiday party. I was happy to be with him but a little sad knowing he wouldn't be proposing that night.

By this time, almost all the snow and ice had quietly melted away. I realized that we wouldn't have a white Christmas after all. It would, however, make the drive to the party much safer.

The gathering was a happy one. My nieces and nephew were a joy to watch as they opened their gifts. Paul and I had a wonderful time with my family. Eventually, after all the gifts had been opened and all goodbyes repeatedly exchanged, we left.

It was a long, quiet ride home, as Paul fell asleep 25 minutes into the trip. The roads were dry and the trees were barren. Yet the stars shone brightly against the black, cloudless sky, adding a touch of beauty to the night.

As I neared my home, a small group of trees caught my attention. They stood out from the rest of the dull, dry landscape. Of all the tress I had passed on my way home, these were the only ones that had any sign of the recent winter storm upon their branches. As I drove, I wondered how this could be. The temperature was much too warm. Yet somehow the branches were covered in an incredible layer of ice. I had seen ice-covered trees many times before, but something about these was extraordinary. This was a dazzling light like I had never seen before.

As I gazed at the beautiful trees, warmth spread through my heart. This was a truly magical moment. No longer was I seeing these winter-decorated branches with the eyes on my face; I now looked upon them with the eyes in my heart and soul. That night—Christmas Eve 1997—the air was clean and crisp, the sky was entirely filled with stars, and the trees...the trees sparkled with diamonds. Thousands and thousands of diamonds.

In my heart I knew this was God's way of answering my prayers. I had needed him to show me that there was a man who thought I was worth a commitment, the commitment that is symbolized by a diamond ring. That Christmas Eve, God covered the trees in diamonds for my eyes and heart to behold. It was his way of showing me that he thought I was special and worthwhile enough for an eternal commitment.

As Paul slept quietly in the seat next to me, completely unaware of the miracle that had taken place, joyous tears of peace and self-worth streamed down my face. I knew that I had found someone who would love me forever, and realizing this was more profound and meaningful than any marriage proposal I could ever receive.

By Cynthia J. Teixeira

It Came Upon a Midnight Clear

It came upon a midnight clear,
That glorious song of old,
From angels bending near the earth
To touch their harps of gold:
"Peace on the earth, good will to men,
From heav'n's all-gracious King."
The world in solemn stillness lay
To hear the angels sing.
Words by Edmund Sears (1810–1876)
Music by Richard S. Willis (1819–1900)

Heaven and Angels Sing

AT THE CHRISTMAS EVE church service, I sat with my two boisterous grandchildren, ages three and five. Their parents sat in front of the church to present a nativity reading titled "Silent Night." They had warned the children to behave. I had warned the children to behave. With scrubbed angelic faces and Christmas wonder in their eyes, they looked like model children posing for a magazine holiday spread. I indulged myself in a few moments of pride.

Alec pinched Aubrey. I was grateful that the organ thundered into the first hymn just then, drowning out her yelp. I grabbed her hand before she could return the pinch. During the Lord's Prayer, Aubrey shredded the program I had given her to color on. The crayons had already rolled under the pew. I watched bits of paper fall on the carpet like snow. I would help her pick it up later, but for now the naughtiness I was allowing kept her occupied and her brother quietly admiring.

We were enjoying an uneasy truce when their parents stood to deliver the reading.

"Mommy!" Alec yelled.

She frowned, and he sat back in his seat.

"Silence," my son said to the congregation. "Think for a moment what that word means to you."

My daughter-in-law signed his words. Earlier that year, she began to use her new signing skills for the benefit of the few hearing-impaired members of our church.

Alec said a naughty word, thankfully too low for many to hear. I scowled at him, shaking my finger and my head. Aubrey grinned. Then she proclaimed, every syllable enunciated perfectly, in a clear voice that carried to far corners of the sanctuary, "Alec is a potty mouth!"

Everyone stared. I was too stunned to speak. My son and his wife looked at each other. But instead of anger, I saw surprise.

My son set aside his script and told another story. He told about their daughter being born profoundly deaf. He talked about four years of hearing aids and speech therapy with no guarantee she would ever learn to speak plainly. He talked about the rugged faith that kept the family praying she would have a normal life.

He said Aubrey's outburst was an answer to prayer: the first perfectly enunciated sentence she had ever spoken.

From the back of the room, a lone voice sang the last line of a beloved Christmas Carol: *Hark! The herald angels sing, Glory to the newborn king.*

While the congregation sang four verses of the unscheduled hymn, my two little angels wiggled in their parents' arms, adding laughter and giggles to the joyful Christmas noise.

By Carol Stigger

Into the Wind

♥   ♥   ♥

*S*HE HADN'T BEEN BORN on the high plains of Wyoming. In fact, even now, after all these months, she still called Pennsylvania home. She was only here because in 1923 that's what wives did: They followed their husbands. And her husband had a powerful yen to homestead in the West. So here she found herself, on the lonely plains of Wyoming.

For the most part, Grete Klein had made friends with the land. Well, maybe not friends, but she was learning its ways and that was the first key to survival in this harsh country. She had even learned to accept her "new" house, but the drafty tar-paper shack rattled with each gust of wind.

The wind. The ever-blowing, good-for-nothing, bitter Wyoming wind. The thief that puffed away the few autumn leaves before she had a chance to savor them. It robbed the children of pleasant play and stole the moisture from the crops.

Grete sighed and stoked the fire in the black majestic cookstove. She smiled as she recalled her mother saying, in heavily accented English, "If you vant to get rich, *mein* daughter, you must schtrike those matches tvice!" Rich? Hardly. Even her mother would be amazed and impressed at the ways Grete

found to economize. Corncobs for fuel. Flour sacks sewn into underwear. Cardboard insoles to cover the holes and extend the life of the children's shoes.

And now Christmas was nearly here. Not that the landscape gave evidence of that. In the predawn light, Grete pushed aside the gunnysack curtaining the kitchen window and gazed out. No soft December snow blanketed the bare dirt. Instead, grim skies of gunmetal gray hovered while the wind howled in swirls of dust. Its icy fingers clawed at the flimsy door, while its frigid breath seeped around the crooked window frames. And all the while, a lone cottonwood tree—their only summer shade—batted its skeletal arms in a field dotted with tumbleweeds too stubborn to blow away. Shivering, Grete turned away.

Christmas. And we can't even spare a tree for the children.

Her children were so young. She knew they carried no memories of holidays back home. Of stately evergreens brushing the ceiling. Of *Grossmutter's* fine, hand-blown glass icicles dripping from its full branches. Of visits from the *Weihnachtsmann,* Father Christmas. Or of a table groaning under the weight of tasty traditional delicacies. Roast goose with potato dumplings. Sauerkraut and noodles. Apple strudel.

Oh, and don't forget all the home-baked desserts with their old-world names. I must teach them to the children.

Names like *Pfeffernüsse, Lebkuchen,* and *Blitzkuchen. Nusstorte, Apfel Pfannkuchen,* and *Schnitzbrot.* Like taking roll call, Grete whispered her favorites one by one. The familiar German words rolled from her tongue, comforting her with their rhythm and taste.

Schnitzbrot. *Fruit bread. Hmmm . . . maybe if I made some substitutions, altered the proportions. . . .*

With an excitement she hadn't felt in a long time, Grete pulled out a saucepan, a wooden spoon, and a large tin bowl. She reached for the carefully hoarded currants and dried peaches. Since the fruit was sweet, maybe the children wouldn't notice that she would have to skimp on sugar. She could spare two eggs and felt lucky to have fresh milk from the cow. But *Schnitzbrot* needed yeast. Grete hesitated.

Do I dare?

She dared. Grete lifted the crock of sourdough starter, her old standby. She had tended it faithfully for months, stirring for four days, adding exact amounts of milk, flour, and sugar each fifth day. It was the foundation for their regular fare of bread, johnnycakes, and biscuits. Why not *Schnitzbrot?* Grete could almost hear her mother say, "Ya, that's right, *mein* Grete. Lean into the vind and you vill arrive vit ease."

Humming *"Stille Nacht"* under her breath, Grete set about stewing, draining, and chopping the fruit. She measured. She mixed. She kneaded until the dough was soft and firm. Grete divided the dough into balls and rolled them like clay between her palms. Instead of the customary loaves, she would make a festive fruit bread wreath for each child. She braided the strips and shaped them into small circles. Covering the dough rings with dishtowels, Grete set them aside to rise near the radiating warmth of the cook stove.

Now, if only the children could have a tree. It would seem more like home. Then I think I could be satisfied.

A Christmas tree. No amount of wishing, no amount of dreaming, no amount of wanting would make it so. Of course, there was still prayer. Doubtfully, Grete closed her eyes and paused a long, silent moment.

Realizing it was nearly time to wake the family, she grabbed her long woolen coat and headed for the door. Let them sleep. She would see to a few outside chores first.

Grete lowered her head to shield her face from the grit of whirling dust. She leaned into the breath-stealing wind, headed toward the barn, and—she gasped when she felt it. As sharp as needles, spiny tentacles pricked her stockings, scratched her legs. Tumbleweeds. Thorny, branched tumbleweeds. Those last, stubborn thistles had finally broken loose in this gale and rolled right to her feet.

With a hoot of laughter, Grete plucked them from around her ankles. She gathered tumbleweeds and carried them gingerly to the house. Already she could imagine her children giggling and stacking to make a towering tumbleweed tree. An answer to prayer. A gift from the fickle Wyoming wind. Who would have thought!

Remembering *Grossmutter*'s heirloom icicles, she felt a fleeting tug of regret. But she shrugged and turned her thoughts toward tissue paper, shiny ribbon, and scraps of cotton batting. The children could string popcorn and make paper chains. Together, they would create new traditions. Perhaps, with a few clicks of her knitting needles and a little more thought, she could even arrange some small gifts from Father Christmas.

And at that very moment, Grete swore she heard her mother whisper, "Yust think, *mein* daughter. First *sauer Schnitzbrot*. And now a Vyoming Christmas tree. Vhat a vonderful place is home."

BY CAROL MCADOO REHME

Caroling

NOTHING WARMS THE HEART quite like Christmas caroling. The holidays can be hectic, and the spirit of Christmas can easily become lost in the rush and worry of getting everything "just right." Last year on the day before Christmas Eve, eight of us decided to take a much-needed break and spend the evening caroling with our children. Setting out with the intention of lifting the spirits of our neighbors, we spread Christmas cheer until we were tired, chilled, and, admittedly, grouchy.

One more house, we decided, and piling into our cars again we spotted the perfect target. The lonely-looking elderly man sitting alone in his kitchen window seemed like he needed us. Pulling over, we parked our cars in front of his house and argued about which songs to sing. Half of the children were either whining or crying about the cold, and the beautiful Utah snow seemed to have lost its sparkle despite our good intentions.

We finally settled on four songs for the man, then rang the bell and waited for him to open his door. Already thinking about getting the kids to bed and the work I had yet to do, I automatically started in on "We Wish You a Merry Christmas" with the others. But as the man stood in the doorway, his eyes filling with tears, my sidetracked thoughts came to a screeching halt. As we sang, I could hear the emotion in many of my friends' voices, and my singing grew softer as I fought the tears myself.

The elderly gentleman stood in his doorway, the kitchen light behind him lighting his soft silver hair like a gentle halo. He clapped with delight as we finished the first song and glided right into the next. Warm air emptied out of his front door, but he didn't seem to care: He was so happy with our visit. He seemed to personify the spirit of Christmas, and I felt a guilty twinge about my grouchiness.

True joy began to fill my soul as I sang my heart out for this man. No one had greeted us with such enthusiasm and joy all night. No one had made us feel so welcome and so loved. Finishing up with "Silent Night," we sang as sweetly and lovingly as we could, and his own shaky voice joined in with us. Tears streamed down my cold cheeks.

Thanking us profusely and wishing us a merry Christmas, he happily went back inside his warm home. We slowly and regrettably left the man, whose spirit and tears made all the difference in our night, all the difference in our Christmas. Although he had sat alone in his window, looking as if he needed us, we had no idea how much we needed him.

BY SUSAN FAHNCKE

Vigil of Hope

❦ ❦ ❦

WE HAD MADE IT THROUGH a rough October fire season with minimal damage. Christmas was now two days away, and the thought of another brushfire near the Cleveland National Forest was the farthest thing from my mind. But when my husband, Rick, a dedicated firefighter, got the call that a fire had broken out on a ridge about ten miles from our home, my stomach went tight.

I took a deep breath and kissed him goodbye as he went off that day to fight what was being described as a small but dangerous fire. Rick assured me that they would tame the blaze in no time and that he would be home the next day for a wonderful Christmas Eve with our three small children.

As I busily made holiday preparations, I kept the TV on, with the volume low enough so as not to disturb the children playing in their rooms. I occasionally peeked at the TV, grateful to see only one short local news update about the fire, which was now under control. I sighed with relief as the reporter on the scene announced that the lack of high winds made the fight a lot easier.

I was sure Rick would be home for dinner, but he called from his cell phone to let me know that they were having trouble with some hot spots—and that he would be home late. At least, he said, the fire was almost completely put out.

Four hours later, I put on the 11 o'clock news and was horrified to see that the top story was the fire, now raging out of control. The reporters on the scene described the situation as grave. Apparently, the winds had kicked up that night and were fanning the hot spots into new fires that converged on an area of extremely dense dried brush. Battalions from all over Southern California were called in to assist, and some were even coming from as far east as Arizona.

My children were in bed, so I sat frozen on the couch watching in horror. When the phone rang, I practically jumped out of my skin. I answered breathlessly, expecting to hear Rick's voice, but it was my sister, Jane, concerned about the fire. She lived in the next town and was on her way over, despite my protests.

I spent all night with my sister and two neighbors, who had come over to be with me as we waited for word. Several nearby towns closer to the forest edge were being evacuated, and I began to wonder if I should prepare overnight bags for the kids. My two neighbors left around 3:00 A.M., but my sister stayed as Christmas Eve day broke without a word from Rick.

By now, the local channels were showing uninterrupted coverage of the fire, which was now spreading at a disastrous rate. Water-dropping planes and choppers with fire retardant were flying constantly overhead on their way to the fire site. My kids were stirring, so Jane went in to help them get dressed as I prepared breakfast, my ears glued to the TV.

I got a call from Rick three hours later. He was on a break, and I could hear his labored breathing through the bad connection. He would not be home for a while, he told me, as his command was going to set backfires on a ridge to try to stop the fire from leaving the National Forest area and jumping a highway. "What a way to spend Christmas Eve day," he laughed, but I didn't hear much humor in his voice.

By late afternoon, dozens of friends and family members had converged on my house. I wasn't sure if I felt better surrounded by loved ones or completely alone in my fear and horror. Still, the noise and human bodies alone served to keep me sane and did wonders for my kids, all of whom were now really frightened. They wanted their daddy home, but they knew he was working hard at a job he loved. For little ones, their wisdom often surprised me, and it certainly gave me strength.

It was a reporter on the local broadcast that broke the terrible news. A crew of ten firefighters had been trapped on a ridge while attempting to set backfires. The winds had changed, and the fire had turned back on them with such speed and fury that flames now surrounded them. I knew in my heart that this was Rick's crew. Jane and I exchanged glances, silently wondering how much worse it could get. I watched the live footage in a state of shock.

A neighbor had thoughtfully taken the kids to McDonald's so they would not have to see what the rest of us were seeing, but I wondered what I would tell them when they returned. How would I tell them that not only was Daddy not coming home for Christmas Eve but that he might never come back at all? The very thought made me ill.

I knew I had to go to him. I knew I could not stand here in my living room, safe and secure, and watch this unfold on TV. I got my purse and coat and headed toward the door. "I'm going to him," I said. Jane leapt into action, calling our neighbor at McDonald's to bring the kids home right away. Jane would bring them in her car. Several friends grabbed their coats and followed me, not wanting me to go alone.

We made a caravan to the edge of the fire site, where several police cars had set up a barricade point. We were about two miles from the western edge of the flames, and we could see the glow of the fire and feel the heat. The police warned us that if the winds changed, we would need to get out of there fast.

But I wasn't going anywhere. I got down on my knees in front of the barricade, and I closed my eyes and prayed. My friends joined me, praying silently beside me. After a long while, I opened my eyes and just sat there, staring straight ahead, silently pleading with God to bring them back alive.

Someone from behind me touched me on the shoulder. I turned to see a woman holding two lighted candles in cups. She handed me one of them and smiled. I saw a strange glow behind her, and for a second I thought the fire had come up behind us, but my heart leapt with joy when I saw dozens—no, hundreds—of people holding candles. My friends and I rose from our knees in awe as a vigil of hope spread out behind us, with dozens more people joining the group every moment. The police looked a little worried at first, but then they, too, took lit candles.

I saw Jane edging her way through the growing crowd, and I couldn't help but cry out when my three kids ran toward me, each holding a vigil light. We hugged and got down on our knees, and we began to pray again, this time out loud. It was a simple prayer, just asking God for protection for the men and women caught on the ridge. When we were finished, we heard a massive chorus of voices respond with "Amen."

For the next two hours, the crowd joined my family in silent prayers, each in their own faith. It didn't matter if they were Christian or Jewish or Buddhist. They were all human beings, drawn together in concern and love for others. I believe it was that unity of faith and strength that caused the winds to die down that night and made it possible for surrounding units to squelch the fire around the ridge where Rick was trapped. And I believe it was the power of prayer that gave my husband and his crew the escape route they needed to make their way down the side of a mountain to safety below.

Another two hours passed before we got word that Rick and the others had made it off the ridge, all ten of them. Three were suffering from smoke inhalation, and another five were being treated for exhaustion, but all were alive. A cheer of happiness and relief went up from the crowd, which had grown even bigger thanks to local news coverage describing the ongoing "Vigil of Hope." As we all hugged each other, strangers and friends alike, it occurred to me that none of us were really strangers after all. Tragedies like this fire on Christmas Eve had a way of bringing together people who might never come together over anything else.

And maybe, just maybe, that was God's plan.

When Rick finally came home on Christmas afternoon, after spending the night in the hospital, I knew that my family had been given the greatest gift of all, an answer to our prayers. We were exhausted, but we were alive, together, and grateful. It was the best Christmas we ever had.

BY M. D. SAVINO

The Tale of Three Trees

❧ ❧ ❧

THREE LITTLE TREES stood high upon a mountain discussing their dreams for the future. The first little tree looked up at the dazzling night sky and said, "I want to carry the treasure of kings and queens. I want to be beautiful. I want to be filled with all the riches in the world."

The nearby stream caught the second little tree's eye. "I want to be a mighty sailing vessel," he said. "I want to sail in the roaring oceans, roam the high seas, and deliver kings and queens safely to their destinations."

The third little tree loved the mountaintop. "I want to stay right here and grow and grow and grow," she said. "I want the people that pass by to look at me touching heaven and think of God."

One day, many years later, three lumberjacks came to help the three trees with the next season of their lives.

The first tree, now beautiful, was cut down. "I will become the most beautiful treasure chest," he thought. "I will get to hold all of the world's riches."

The mighty second tree was cut down. "I will now sail the roaring oceans," thought the second tree. "I will be the mightiest of all sailing vessels."

The third tree, with her branches stretched toward heaven, was also cut down. Together with the other two trees, she was taken down the lovely hillside.

The first tree arrived at a carpenter's shop. The beautiful tree was aglow with excitement. But he wasn't made into a treasure chest. The skillful car-

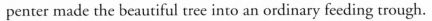

penter made the beautiful tree into an ordinary feeding trough.

The second tree was brought to a shipyard. The mighty second tree thought, "Now I will be the most vigorous of vessels." But the strong second tree was made into a simple little fishing boat.

The third tree was brought to a lumberyard. There she was made into beams and put aside. "Why did this happen?" thought the third tree. "All I ever wanted was to touch heaven."

As the weeks passed, their dreams began to fade from memory. However, one magical night brought the first tree's dream to life. A young mother put her newborn into the trough. "This manger is perfect," said the mother to her husband. And the first tree knew he was cradling the most important treasure ever.

One night the fishing boat was used by a tired traveler and his friends. They quickly fell asleep, and the small boat floated out to sea. The sea became rough, and a thunderstorm was brewing. This frightened the second tree. If only he were a mighty vessel and could withstand the force of the storm! The traveler was awakened by the storm, and he stretched out his arms and said, "Peace." The sea became calm and the thunderstorm vanished. It was then that the second tree realized he was carrying the Almighty King.

On a Friday morning, the third tree was taken by soldiers and carried through a hostile mob. She trembled with fear and distaste as a man's hands were nailed to her. But the following Sunday the sun rose. The earth was full of joy. She realized that everything had changed because of God's love.

The first tree was made beautiful.

The second tree was made mighty.

The third tree made people think of God.

The Truth About Santa

THE CHILDREN WERE finally nestled all snug in their beds. The stockings were hung and the prayers had been said. I had notions of getting some sleep myself, but I couldn't start to fill the stockings if there was even the slightest chance that one of our little ones was awake. All five of them still believed in Santa, and I didn't want to spoil that.

I could remember when I learned the truth about Santa. I was seven, just about my son Mike's age, when I found the store wrappings from Betsy Wetsy in the trash after I'd found her in my stocking. I knew then that my parents were the ones responsible for our Christmas surprises.

I tiptoed up the stairs to make sure the children were asleep. Little Lisa had dozed off during church and Frank had carefully carried her up to her crib. She looked like a cherub curled up with her bunny blankie.

Big sister Becky was sound asleep, too. She had hurried up to bed hoping that Santa would fill her stocking first. At six, she was our staunchest believer. Not a single doubt about Santa's existence crept into her explanations of how he got to all the children in the world. "His reindeer fly really, really fast," she'd say. I pulled her covers up. She didn't stir.

I peeked into our room as I passed. Frank was sleeping peacefully without a trace of guilt that he'd left me to wait up to fill stockings. He had, after all, laid the fire so it would be ready to light in the morning.

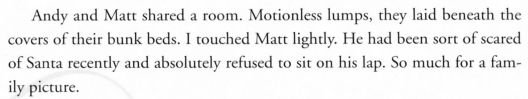

Andy and Matt shared a room. Motionless lumps, they laid beneath the covers of their bunk beds. I touched Matt lightly. He had been sort of scared of Santa recently and absolutely refused to sit on his lap. So much for a family picture.

Andy was surrounded by trucks, his favorite bedtime buddies. I kissed his cheek. His nose was still a little rosy from his role as Rudolph in the preschool sing-along. I had to be sure that Andy didn't see me doing Santa's duties. He'd be dreadfully disappointed.

I snuck silently into Mike's room. He was my skeptic. Several of his second grade friends had tried to convince him that there was no real Santa. He was wavering. I hoped he'd hang on to his belief for at least one more Christmas. Maybe by next year I'd have a better plan for handling his moment of truth. I tapped him gently. "Mikey, are you still awake?" Mike didn't answer.

I looked at his clock: 11:30. It seemed safe to start. With one ear tuned to the upstairs, I started five piles on the dining room table. I began organizing: Apples for everybody, toothbrushes to counteract the chocolate marshmallow snowmen, and boxes of fancy bandages. Becky would love her Barbie ones. For the boys, I added little metal airplanes—just like the kind Frank flew. I went into the kitchen and took the bag of specially requested toys from the top shelf of the cupboard. I carefully removed the price tags and tossed the wrappings into the trash compactor. I wouldn't leave behind any evidence.

Suddenly, I heard the squeak of small feet on the stairs. I turned around quickly. There stood Mike, eyes as big as Christmas bulbs. His lower lip trembled. "So what the kids said is true," he said sadly. "It's just you and Dad that fill stockings. Santa isn't real. . . ."

At a loss for words, I hugged my small son. Then I attempted an explanation. "Santa is real, Mike. He's as real as love and laughter, secrets and surprises, magic and memories."

That sounded good, so I continued. "Sometimes children are disappointed when they discover that Santa lives in people's hearts, not at the North Pole. They want to believe that the toys they find on Christmas morning are made in Santa's workshop rather than picked out by parents. Becky and the kids aren't ready to learn that, so I hope you won't tell them."

"I won't," promised Mike.

I continued. "Santa is lots and lots of people who keep the spirit of Christmas alive."

Mike's face brightened a bit. "Are just parents Santa Claus?"

I hesitated a moment. "Santa can be anybody, I guess."

"Could I be part of Santa?" he asked solemnly.

"I don't see why not," I answered. "This year, why don't you stuff the apples into the toes of the stockings."

Proudly, he pushed them in. "Next year maybe Becky will be ready to be a helper," he said. "I won't tell her, but I can't wait till she finds out the truth about Santa, too."

"Run on up to bed now," I encouraged after he finished the apples. "It's my turn to be Santa."

Giggling as he headed up the stairs, Mike waved and whispered, "Happy Christmas to all, and to all a good night."

BY ELLEN JAVERNICK

The Stoic

I HAVE WEPT in the best places in the United States. I wept in Luray Caverns when they played "Shenandoah" on the organ. I wept in the Barbara Frietchie house when I thought of that grand gal hanging the Stars and Stripes from her window right over Stonewall Jackson's head. And I wept in Independence Hall when I heard a recording of the Liberty Bell.

I have cried tears of joy at every wedding I have ever attended (including my own), and I've wept every time a brand-new baby has been placed in my arms. I even cry almost any time I hear a John Denver song.

My husband, while just as foolishly sentimental as I am, manages to hide the tears. I call him a closet weeper.

Our kids make no particular secret that they are weepers. The boys dash impatiently at their tears, laughing ruefully at themselves. The girls have gone through many a box of tissues while reading *Little Women* or watching a poignant movie . . . but not our third child, Art.

From babyhood, Art has been a stoic. He just can't fathom what makes us all so emotional; he can't see the logic of tears. If he gets hurt, he'll bite his lip to keep from wailing. He'll come for a bandage or even a hug, but he will never cry.

When Art was six years old, our family discovered a Christmas song, "The Littlest Angel," recorded by Bing Crosby. It tells the story of an angel only four years old whose greatest pleasure is playing with the contents of a little box God had graciously allowed him to bring from earth. The box contains, among other things, a butterfly with golden wings and the leash of his faithful dog. According to the song, when the holy child was born in Bethlehem, the heavenly host planned magnificent gifts to honor the occasion. The littlest angel gave the one thing he treasured above all others. You guessed it, the little box and its earthly treasures.

The song became a family lullaby over the years, and it could reduce me to tears in a nanosecond. Despite—or perhaps because of—its tear-jerking quality, the kids loved it, too.

One December, we began singing Christmas carols while we were making cookies. I rolled out the cookie dough and cut it into Christmas trees and stars and bells and angels, and the kids brushed them with beaten eggs and sprinkled them with sugar and cinnamon and chopped nuts. I started singing "The Littlest Angel." The kids listened, wiping their eyes as they brushed, sprinkled, or chopped. The sorrow was strangely comforting as together we worked and I sang. Then, all at once, we hit a snag. The line slowed to a stop. I looked up and saw that the cinnamon jar lay on its side unattended.

"Who's supposed to be sprinkling cinnamon?" I asked through my tears.

"Art is, Mom," Kevin sobbed.

"Where is he?"

"Upstairs in our room," Kevin sniffed.

"Well, go get him."

Ruthie took over sugar and cinnamon duties while Kevin ran upstairs to fetch Art. In a few minutes, he returned alone.

"He's crying, Mom," he said incredulously. "He says that he just hates it when you sing that song; it always makes him cry."

A closet weeper, just like his father!

"Jingle bells, jingle bells," I sang at the top of my lungs.

In another few minutes, Art reappeared and picked up the cinnamon jar.

You just don't kiss the stoic in front of the whole family. But, oh, sometimes you want to.

By MILLIE BAKER RAGOSTA

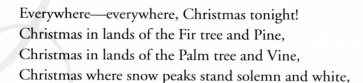

Everywhere—everywhere, Christmas tonight!
Christmas in lands of the Fir tree and Pine,
Christmas in lands of the Palm tree and Vine,
Christmas where snow peaks stand solemn and white,

Christmas where cornfields stand sunny and
bright . . . Christmas where peace, like a dove in its flight
Broods o'er brave men in the thick of the fight;
Everywhere, everywhere, Christmas tonight!
PHILLIP BROOKS, *The Meaning of Christmas*

No Santa

"WHAT A DUMMY," Danny said, sneering directly in my face. "What a great big dummy." The other kids joined him in laughing at me, pointing fingers, telling me how incredibly stupid I was.

"You can't really still believe in Santa Claus?" asked Elizabeth, who was pretty much my best friend—in some ways my only friend.

I felt the hot flush of shame flood my face. Confronted by Danny and the others, I realized just how slow and stupid I'd been. I wasn't some tiny kid, either. I was old enough to know better than to believe in fairytales.

I rushed from the playground into school and fought all day to keep my head up and the blushes from my cheeks. How could I be so stupid?

Oh, how I had believed. Never a year passed that I wasn't peering from my bedroom window, watching for him, anxious to hear sleigh bells on the roof, eager for a glimpse of him, just once. I spent hours staring out into the night, watching and waiting. I was even half-scared that I would see Santa, that I'd spoil the whole thing by seeing him when I wasn't supposed to.

In my excitement, on Christmas Eve each year, I struggled to be good, to stay in bed, to close my eyes and fall promptly to sleep. But excitement and the mystery of it all kept me awake.

And when I heard rustling down the hall, I held my breath and ducked my head beneath the covers. I wouldn't peek. I wouldn't spoil the magic. Thus, it

hit me hard when I realized I'd been fooled all those years, misled, lied to. My grandmother, my parents, all those kind-eyed adults who urged me to write letters to Santa about my heart's desires—they all deceived me.

For days I felt cheated, so disappointed that I felt like crying for my loss and unhappiness. Part of me felt rage, too, that so many people had lied to me, that they'd allowed me to trust something false, that they'd left me standing like a fool when Danny shattered my beliefs.

But I wasn't a tiny kid. I was old enough to pay attention and to think it through. It hit me then. If there was no Santa, none, never, then all those special Christmases, all those wonderful gifts, all those blessings—all of it came from Mom and Dad. I thought of how tight the budget had been in some of those years, how difficult it must have been for my parents.

A feeling of awe came over me. No Santa. No magic. No unlimited funds from the North Pole and elves creating toys. That meant Mom and Dad scrimped and saved. Mom and Dad made the magic for us. Mom and Dad loving us so much that they'd made endless sacrifices and expected no thanks, no reward, no appreciation.

I felt astounded at all they'd done. So much amazing love all those years. And just like that I understood. That's what Christmas was all about—the sort of love that gives and gives and gives. I understood about God giving us his very best, his son. I understood about Mom and Dad giving us their very best, their love wrapped in huge, wonderful, exciting packages.

And I didn't need to believe in Santa anymore. No more fantasies. I had discovered the real thing instead—and it was just as good.

By Karen M. Leet

In Swaddling Clothes

❧   ❧   ❧

AFTER THEY HAD wrapped up the baby in a blanket and drove him away in a police car, I felt relieved. They would take the kid to a hospital and check him out, feed him a bottle of formula, and dress him in warm clothes. "Baby John Doe," as the police called him, would be safe and sound.

Sergeant Loomis pulled up a chair at my kitchen table. "Our next job is to find out everything we can so that we can begin looking for the mother," he said. The police officer flipped open his notebook.

"Where should I start?" I asked.

"How about when you left the house?"

"Well, I left right after I finished dinner—around seven, I guess."

"Was anyone else here at the time?"

"No. I'm divorced. My daughter used to live with me, but she moved out a few months ago. She got married."

He probably noticed the scowl on my face, but he didn't say anything. I continued.

"I always take Goldie for a walk right after I eat, so I put on her leash and we started out. It was snowing. I remember thinking it was colder than I'd expected.

"Anyway, I usually turn right and walk Goldie down Walnut Street, but tonight I decided to go by St. Elizabeth's instead."

"Why?"

"Well, it's Christmas Eve. I could hear them singing 'Silent Night.' I guess I should have gone to the service, but I wasn't in the right frame of mind, so I thought maybe I'd at least hear some of the carols."

"Okay. So you walked your dog down to the church. Then what happened?"

"I just stood there listening for a while—maybe five minutes. I could hear parts of the Christmas Eve service. I was remembering other years, thinking about how the service would go. Reverend Kilmer would tell how Jesus was born in Bethlehem and how the angels announced it to the shepherds, who were out on the hills, tending their flocks: 'And ye shall find the babe, wrapped in swaddling clothes, lying in a manger. . . .' That used to be my daughter's favorite part of the story."

"And then?"

"That's when I noticed someone in the alley. Whoever it was rushed away when they saw me."

"Can you tell me anything about the person you saw? Was it a man or a woman? How tall? What were they wearing?"

"I'm sorry. At the time I didn't know it was going to be important, so I wasn't really paying attention. I was thinking about some . . . some family matters."

The officer frowned. "That could have been the mother, or someone else connected with the baby, who came out of the alley."

"Yes, I know," I said apologetically.

"Go on with your story."

"Then I heard a high, thin sound—a baby crying in the alley between the church and Blake's Department Store. Goldie started whining and tugging on her leash. She led me over to a Dumpster.

"It wasn't hard to find the baby. Someone had left him on a heap of trash bags and broken-up cardboard boxes. I could tell he was a newborn. He was wrapped in that dingy white bath towel I showed you. His little face was already turning blue from the cold, so I unbuttoned my coat and put him inside. Then I ran home with him and called the police."

Sergeant Loomis looked at me carefully. "Have you noticed any young girl in the neighborhood lately who might have been expecting a baby?"

A sudden panicked thought made me hesitate before answering. "No. I . . . I'm not around here much. I'm a truck driver—mainly short haul, but sometimes I'm gone for a few days. I don't have any real friends in the neighborhood. Mrs. Riggs next door is the only neighbor I talk to. She takes care of Goldie when I'm not home."

"Well, here's my card. If you remember any details you think would help us, give me a call."

"Uh, wait a minute, Sergeant." I felt like a sentimental fool, but I couldn't help asking. "Would it be okay if I visited the kid in the hospital? Just so I can see if he's doing all right?"

Loomis smiled. "They took him to the neonatal ward at St. Joseph's. You know where that is? Just a few blocks from here."

"Yeah. Thanks."

I waited until I was positive Sergeant Loomis had driven away. Then I raced to the phone and dialed a familiar number.

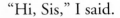

"Hi, Sis," I said.

"Richard! I thought you didn't want anything to do with us!"

"Yeah, well. I was just calling to find out if Jennie had the baby yet."

"No, but it could happen any day now. She's doing fine. She and Brian are so excited! They've got the nursery all ready. Would you like to talk to her?"

"Uh, no. Not right now." I wrapped up the conversation quickly, feeling guilty and relieved at the same time. Maybe I should have talked to Jennie, but I wasn't ready for that. Not yet. At least I knew that the poor abandoned baby wasn't hers.

Although the falling snow was beautiful, the wind was bitter. Shivering, I pulled up the hood of my parka. Yes, I thought, that tiny boy wrapped in nothing but a ragged towel definitely had a close call tonight.

The neighborhood was festooned with garlands of evergreen and strings of multicolored lights. Christmas trees twinkled in living room windows. Late as it was, people were still coming and going from holiday get-togethers, laughing and chattering as they climbed out of cars or knocked on their friends' front doors. The children's voices reminded me of how excited Jennie used to get on Christmas Eve, when she was a little girl—which didn't seem so long ago.

When I asked at the nurses' desk about the abandoned baby boy, a motherly looking RN assured me that he was doing fine. "Come with me, and you can have a peek at him," she offered.

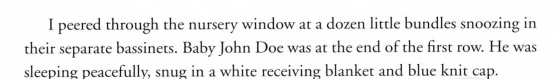

I peered through the nursery window at a dozen little bundles snoozing in their separate bassinets. Baby John Doe was at the end of the first row. He was sleeping peacefully, snug in a white receiving blanket and blue knit cap.

"It's hard to believe somebody would just throw him away," I said after a while. "I don't understand a woman who would do that."

"Maybe she wasn't a woman," the nurse answered gently. "Maybe she was just a girl—scared, with no family or friends to turn to. I agree it wasn't the right thing to do, but raising a baby is a big responsibility. Some girls aren't ready to take it on, so they panic."

"I have a daughter, Jennie, who's only 17. She's expecting a baby any day now. She dated Brian for over a year, and when she found out she was pregnant they decided to get married." I glanced over at the nurse, but she said nothing.

I continued. "I was so disappointed—so angry at her. You see, the same thing happened to me when I was still in high school. I married my girlfriend—Jennie's mother—and we tried to make it work, but we were just too young, and no one helped us. I wanted to go to college, but I never even finished high school. To top it all off, my wife left me. I raised Jennie alone from when she was a toddler."

"You didn't want Jennie to have a rough time of it, to give up all her plans and possibly ruin her life," the nurse said.

"That's right. I see now that I should have been there for her, ready to help her make the right decision—whatever that is. But I wasn't. I told her if she got married and raised the baby, I didn't want anything to do with her. I hoped that would bring her to her senses—make her realize that raising a baby at her age was foolish.

"Tonight when I found that little boy who was left to freeze in an alley, I knew that whatever else you can say about Jennie, the decision she made was a responsible one."

"A loving one," the nurse said with a smile. "She grew up with a good example to follow—yours."

"I wish I believed that," I said. "At least my sister was there. Her family took Jennie and Brian in."

We stood together in silence for a moment more. Then the nurse said, "Let me predict a happy ending to the story of Jennie and Brian and their baby. I don't think they'll lose sight of their dreams and ambitions. I think they're going to have plenty of family support." She looked at me, and, it seemed, right through me. "Don't you agree, Grandpa?"

Maybe it was Baby John Doe, or maybe because it was Christmas Eve, but my heart was suddenly full of hope. I left the hospital to make the long-over-due phone call.

"Jennie? . . . It's Dad." I knew I caught her off guard, but I forged ahead. "Can I come over tomorrow—and spend Christmas with you . . . and Brian? Or, both of you could come here." It was a good beginning.

When I hung up, I smiled contentedly. My new son-in-law and my wonderful, responsible daughter were coming home. And I was going to be a grandfather! It just doesn't get much better than that.

BY RICHARD MASON, AS TOLD TO ANN RUSSELL

The Midnight Hour

❧ ❧ ❧

"*TU SCENDI DELLA NOTTE*" still reverberates in my ears, without the music, without the choir, without the candlelight. It still brings tingles to my arms and tears to my eyes. I can still hum the refrain and hear it boom with deep baritones. All of the singers had dark, thick hair, deep chocolate eyes, and soft, chiseled features. All were Italian. Some spoke English, some didn't. All that mattered was that they could sing. And sing they did!

"Tootsie Roll, are you looking forward to church?" my grandma asked that Christmas Eve day.

"Yes, Grammy," I affirmed. Normally, I hated the Latin mass—it seemed to last forever. But midnight mass—that was different. It never lasted long enough.

First, though, came our traditional Christmas Eve dinner: soup, several kinds of fish prepared every way imaginable, pasta, grizpelis—which were donuts twisted into whatever shape Gram created—and a little red wine.

"Manga, manga!" Gram would say. Eat, eat! This feast was prepared for the multitudes who simply dropped in because they knew they would be fed. And never did anyone walk away from the table hungry.

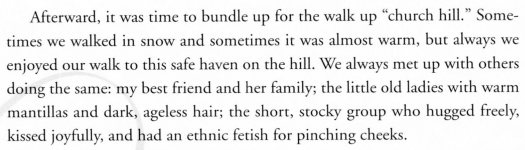

Afterward, it was time to bundle up for the walk up "church hill." Sometimes we walked in snow and sometimes it was almost warm, but always we enjoyed our walk to this safe haven on the hill. We always met up with others doing the same: my best friend and her family; the little old ladies with warm mantillas and dark, ageless hair; the short, stocky group who hugged freely, kissed joyfully, and had an ethnic fetish for pinching cheeks.

We all filed into the tiny brick structure with stained glass windows, filled with smells of pine and glittering with ornaments. The church seemed to sway on the hill with the melodic symphony of deep, rich male voices singing old-world songs with the original, precious Italian words.

We squeezed into those hard-backed pews and settled in for a peaceful hour, which gave us acceptance of yesterday, appreciation for today, and hope for tomorrow. We were shoulder to shoulder with love and tradition, warmth and togetherness. Ethnic bonding existed; we knew who we were. That mass was exuberant, as the music overpowered even the thickly engraved wooden doors.

"Grammy, how can they sing without music?"

"They *are* the music," she assured me as she cupped my chin in her soft, firm, gentle hand. And they were. These men who sang *a cappella* needed nothing to back them up except the symphony of appreciation that surrounded them and us as we drifted off to Naples or Calabria or Umberto. *"Tu scendi della notte."* To this day, the words warm my heart.

BY ELIZABETH TOOLE

Picture Perfect

❧   ❧   ❧

I T WAS BITTER and barren on the dry, windswept plains that December of 1885. And it was nearly as bleak inside the humble home of the Endicott family.

They had literally built their house from the Kansas earth itself, harvesting heavy clumps of root-packed dirt and mortaring them to make walls. Even the roof was nothing more than thick prairie grass springing from hand-cut slabs.

It was a one-room house, a sod house.

Never mind that the family shared it with spiders, centipedes, and a host of other insects. Never mind that mice scurried inside the cheesecloth ceiling or that an occasional bull snake slithered down the lodge-pole frame. Never mind that when it stormed outside, inside it dripped rain and oozed mud. Never mind that with each gust of the biting wind, dust sifted through the cracks of the rough-hewn doorframe.

It was their home, and the Endicotts were grateful for it.

The family was coming off a rough year. The summer drought had nearly taken their crop, and the greedy prairie fire finished it off. Yet they had much to be thankful for. They knew the family would eat this winter, as the hens were still laying and the milk cow was still wet. And, although it "went against his grain," Pa had set up a line of credit with Mr. Ellis down at the General Mercantile in town—for the good of his family.

Although they would have to burn their meager fuel supply sparingly, they knew the walls of the sod house were 14 inches thick—fine insulation against the raging winter blizzards that were bound to hit later. Moreover, the entire family was fit and healthy.

Now the holiday season was upon them. Even though there was little means, the Endicotts were determined to do their best with what they had and to celebrate their blessings.

"It will be a perfect Christmas," Pa promised. "Just you wait and see."

With mufflers leaving only their dancing eyes exposed, the bundled children followed Pa to the creek bottom. Together they selected and cut down a puny, winter-bare sapling and took turns dragging it home along the frozen ground. Once it was secured in an empty molasses bucket and their fingers had thawed out, Ma showed them how to make decorations.

They linked paper chains—torn from narrow strips of carefully hoarded newspaper—with a thin paste Ma had stirred together from flour and water. They poked fluffy white kernels with Ma's sewing needles as they strung fragrant popcorn to drape the branches. Pa even produced a small meadowlark nest he had been saving for "just the right occasion" and tucked it securely on a forked twig. One and all, they agreed that this year's was the "prettiest tree ever."

Finally, they gathered in front of the smoky, open hearth. It was time for presents.

Pa played Santa Claus and was greeted with squeals of delight over the elaborate selection. The girls cooed over velvet hair ribbons, music boxes, and porcelain-faced dolls with shiny black shoes. The boys' eyes grew bright at the sight of shiny traps, double-barreled shotguns, and a variety of new pocketknives.

Ma fingered her ready-made bonnets, inspected the cast-iron stove, and clicked her tongue over frivolous kid gloves. Pa admired the fancy hand-tooled saddle Ma passed to him. And everyone laughed over the *seven* pairs of long johns he received because they all knew "a man don't need more than he can wear at any one time."

It was an extravagant Christmas for the Endicott family. And each hand-picked surprise had come straight from the Montgomery Ward Catalog. Oh, not mail order as might be expected. After all, the entire Endicott family knew they couldn't afford that. No, these gifts had come *straight* from the worn catalog.

The Endicotts had fingered through the tattered book, one page at a time. They were generous in their dreams, meticulous in their selections, and eager in their efforts to please. Then, using Ma's sharp embroidery scissors, they neatly clipped out each gift. It was those snippets of paper, those little black and white pictures, the family now cherished.

Pa had made good on his promise. Christmas *was* perfect. Picture perfect.

By Carol McAdoo Rehme

Our Christmas Guest

CHRISTMAS WOULDN'T BE Christmas without remembering the early-morning phone call. I opened my eyes just enough to know that it was still pitch-black outside and that, yes, the phone was ringing. Two thoughts immediately rushed through my mind: One, the ringing would wake up the many guests in our house, and two... what was wrong?

My groggy "Hello" was greeted by a chipper, "Merry Christmas, Elaine. This is Vivian!"

Vivian! It was Vivian—that special lady who had decided to call herself my other mom because my mother lived out of state. Over the years, she had often made a telephone call or sent a card or gift. She had almost a supernatural timing—always knowing when her love and reassurance was needed.

Early in December, I had been in a hospital intensive-care unit recovering from surgery for a brain tumor. There I learned that my friend, Vivian, had been sent home from the hospital to die. As long as she could handle the pain, home was where she wanted to be. The cancer had spread throughout her body, and sometimes just sitting in the chair for a short time took all the energy she had. But now in the dark, her voice sounded strong, and she said, "I'm coming over to see you. I want to see for myself that you are all right."

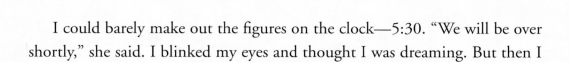

I could barely make out the figures on the clock—5:30. "We will be over shortly," she said. I blinked my eyes and thought I was dreaming. But then I heard the phone click, and I put the receiver back into place.

We dressed quickly and were surprised to see that the phone had not awakened anyone else. At six o'clock on Christmas morning, my husband and I sat across from Vivian and her husband at our kitchen table. She wore a purple turban to hide her baldness. Her red silk blouse hung loosely now on her frail shoulders. But her eyes sparkled, and her smile was radiant.

"They told me that the Lord gave you a miracle," she said. "I can see now that he has. I just wanted one more time to see his wondrous works. You know, very soon he is going to take all this pain of mine away, and I will have my miracle, too."

With that declaration of faith, she reached into her purse and pulled out her two favorite Christmas tree ornaments. "They are yours now," she uttered. With that, she burst forth into singing Christmas carols with such gusto that we all sat in amazement. Then we joined in, and for the next 30 minutes we sang and laughed. "This is our very own special Christmas party, Elaine!" she said.

We hugged each other, both knowing that it was for the last time. Then she and her husband were gone. I went back to bed, smiling, knowing that the real spirit of Christmas—one of God's own—had just been our Christmas guest.

BY ELAINE SLATER REESE

The Spirit of Giving

BUT I AM SURE that I have always thought of Christmas time, when it has come round ... as a good time; a kind, forgiving, charitable, pleasant time; the only time I know of, in the long calendar of the year, when men and women seem by one consent to open their shut-up hearts freely.

CHARLES DICKENS
A Christmas Carol

The Furnace Man

❦　❦　❦

I STOOD IN FRUSTRATION in the living room, surrounded by boxes of Christmas decorations. Even my sweatshirt and jacket failed to disguise the fact that the temperature in our house was dropping each hour. The wind continued to whistle outside, and I wondered how much longer it would be before the furnace repairman would show up. Finally, after I had resorted to a pair of gloves (and had given up trying to tie bows with chilled fingers), the doorbell rang.

The appearance of the fellow standing behind my frosted storm door was not necessarily reassuring. I was certainly dressed for the December day more appropriately than he was. On second look, I realized that he was probably dressed as well as his finances would allow. His oily hair blew in the wind.

With a slight limp, his small frame moved from room to room, up and down the basement steps, and back and forth to the thermostat. Obviously, he was a quiet one. I went back to the boxes and started pulling out tinsel and glittered ornaments. Then, as he walked through the living room, he stopped suddenly and stared at me. With a haunting tone in his voice, he said, "We don't celebrate Christmas at our house no more!" It was one of the few times in my 40 years that I could think of nothing to say.

The silence became louder, so I said "oh" and hastily bent down to take the nativity scene out of the box. He retreated down to the basement. Soon, he came up and stated that he had found the problem. He tinkered with the thermostat again . . . then stared at me some more. My eyes met his. "We don't have Christmas at our house no more!" This time, there was an urgency in his voice. I knew what I had to say, but the word was not easy to speak. "Why?"

With my "why," his face changed—a look I couldn't understand—and he stared at me again. Then he stared into space. I could tell he was trying to speak. He started slowly. "My wife and me ain't never had much money, and we had no kids. Then very late in life, we had a little boy." He paused, and his face lit up. His eyes sparkled. "Such a beautiful little boy."

His voice trailed off, and I don't think he even realized that he had slumped down into the chair—as if his legs would no longer support him. I knew then that the boxes could wait. Something about this man in his greasy work clothes on my white, velvet upholstered chair demanded my total attention.

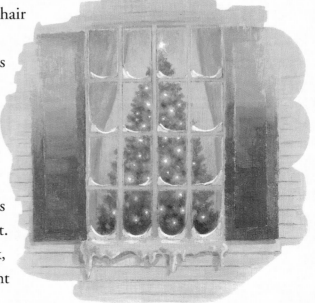

"Why don't you and your wife celebrate Christmas anymore?"

A red flush moved slowly over his face. But as he spoke, I sensed his relief at sharing his pain. I knew that for him, it was easier to share his heavy burden with a complete stranger—one who might not judge.

"My wife and little boy, he was three then, they was crossing a street. A trailer truck stopped for the light. Then, when they was in the middle of the crosswalk, for no reason, he pushed the accelerator and drove right into them."

The pain in his voice tore at my heart. He went on to explain how they had gotten rid of what little furniture they had. Their hurt was so great. They wanted nothing to remind them of their past joy with their son—now gone.

They now had a small table, two chairs, and a mattress on the floor. He pulled out his wallet and showed me that he had almost enough saved to buy a new bed for his crippled wife. I looked at the numerous boxes in my living room, thought of the stacks of wrapped gifts in the basement, and realized that, for a moment, I was part of a world I had never before experienced.

By the time he next came up the steps, my three sons—Rob, Chris, and Blake—were home from school, sitting around the kitchen table with Christmas cookies and milk. I saw the man stand quietly at the top of the steps and watch them. There was no expression on his face. He handed me the bill and started packing up his equipment. I wrote the check, remembering my anger several hours before at knowing I had to come up with extra money at Christmastime for the furnace repair.

I hurried to the stack of wrapped gifts and found one that I had spent hours making. It was my favorite and was for a special friend. I tore the sticker off and replaced it with one that said, "Somebody cares!" A friend had just given me several dozen beautiful Christmas cookies—the kind that are dainty and take hours to decorate. I wrapped the cookies quickly and took them with the present out to the truck.

I handed the man the check and said, "When you go home tonight, tell your wife somebody does care. We care. God cares. I do understand why you don't want to celebrate Christmas anymore, but the real meaning of Christmas is still there."

At first he refused the gifts, then hesitatingly reached out for them. Again his eyes pierced mine. Then the tears welled up and ran down, almost appearing to instantly freeze on his whiskers. He spoke. "Lady, there ain't never been nobody cared about my wife and me. There ain't nobody ever gave us nothing." Then a smile crossed his face. "Now I can give my wife a present for Christmas." He backed the truck out of the driveway as I stood there brushing the tears from my eyes.

At 11:00 that night, our phone rang. The voice on the line was hesitant. "This is the furnace man's wife. I hope you won't mind my calling. I just had to call you. Nobody never done nothing for me and my husband before. My husband told me about your house. He said it looked just like the White House."

I thought of her lying on the mattress on the floor—and my boxes and boxes of decorations and gifts—and understood how he must have described our home to her.

"My husband told me about your three little boys," she continued. "He told me how beautiful they are. He told me about their smiles. Ma'am, would you do one more thing for us? Go upstairs and give each of those little boys a big hug from us. Tell them Merry Christmas and that we love them." And with a big sob, she hung up.

Through my tears, I looked across the room at the plaque on our wall: "Be not forgetful to entertain strangers, for some have thereby entertained angels unawares. (Hebrews 13:2)."

By Elaine Slater Reese

The Christmas Dress

❧   ❧   ❧

MONEY WAS TIGHT that Christmas—not that it wasn't tight much of the time for Tim and Laura with a young family to care for and seemingly endless bills to pay. Still, they both wanted to help their friend, James. Single, studying for the ministry, struggling to get through school on a budget far tighter than theirs, James was always glad to visit their home for dinner, play a few games of Scrabble, and take some leftovers home.

They'd talked it over, figured their finances carefully, prayed about it, and finally decided to provide as generous a cash gift for their friend as they could possibly manage. It might mean a bit less for them, but they felt somehow it was important to help James through this difficult time in his life. He was a good friend, a person full of faith and commitment, a loyal and kind-natured young man.

So, they felt pleased with their decision, excited, full of anticipation.

"I can hardly wait to see his face," Laura whispered as they tucked the cash inside a Christmas card. She didn't even think of what she might have done with that cash herself. She and Tim each felt certain that this was how God wanted them to use the money, to help out a friend rather than spend it on themselves.

They had speculated about how their friend might spend his extra money. Perhaps he'd buy some basic food for his pantry or a sturdy pair of shoes to

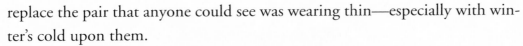

replace the pair that anyone could see was wearing thin—especially with winter's cold upon them.

Tim cautioned Laura not to try to guess what James would do with their gift. "Remember," he told her, "that's between him and God. It's not up to us to choose what James uses the money for."

But in his heart, Tim couldn't resist wondering, too. Was there some great need this money might help meet? Perhaps help with school costs or books? Maybe even help pay the rent for James's tiny place?

Then it was time to present their gift. Laura couldn't stop grinning as James opened the envelope. She loved the look of amazed delight on their friend's face. Tim felt glad that they could help ease the financial pressure on their friend.

James hugged Laura so hard that she could hardly breathe.

"You don't know what this means to me," he told them. "You are so gracious."

Their hearts were full of true Christmas spirit that night.

Feeling wonderful about how they'd helped their friend, Tim and Laura couldn't help feeling stunned when James confided in them how he'd decided to use their gift.

"I'm going to buy my sister a dress," James beamed.

Tim and Laura felt their hearts sink. A dress? Not even something for himself? Not even something he desperately needed, like shoes or decent clothes? Not even food? They couldn't help the feeling of dismay that gripped them both. Their hard-earned money going to buy a dress for James's sister? It didn't seem right. Could that be what God intended? They tried hard not to let their disappointment show.

James didn't seem to notice their reservations, their distress over his choice. Words poured from him. "My sister won't come to church," he went on. "She doesn't feel she has nice enough clothes to wear. She thinks she wouldn't fit in if she didn't have a decent dress on. If she has a nice dress, she'll come. It's the thing I want most in the world."

He hugged them both again. Tim and Laura felt ashamed of themselves, of their dismay, of their doubt. God was using their sacrificial gift in a way they'd never imagined, in a way that would bring more joy than they'd ever thought possible.

James brought his sister to church that Christmas. She wore her new dress proudly week after week, and she ultimately gave her life to God. Their gift had turned her life around. And they had thought it was only a dress.

BY KAREN M. LEET

THE GIFT OF CHRISTMAS

His eyes—how they twinkled! his dimples how merry!
His cheeks were like roses, his nose like a cherry!
His droll little mouth was drawn up like a bow,
And the beard of his chin was as white as the snow.

CLEMENT C. MOORE (1779–1863)
"A VISIT FROM ST. NICHOLAS"

The Christmas Angels

IT WAS DECEMBER 23, 1993. For a single mom who was going to college and supporting my children completely alone, Christmas was looking bleak. I looked around my little home, realization dawning like a slow, twisting pain. We were poor.

Our tiny house had two bedrooms, both off the living room. They were so small that my baby daughter's crib barely fit into one room, and my son's twin bed and dresser were squeezed into the other. There was no way they could share a room, so I made my bed every night on the living room floor. The three of us shared the only closet in the house. We were snug, always only a few feet from each other, day and night. With no doors on the children's rooms, I could see and hear them at all times. It made them feel secure, and it made me feel close to them—a blessing I wouldn't have had in other circumstances.

It was early evening, about 8:00. The snow was falling softly, silently, and my children were both asleep. I was wrapped in a blanket, sitting at the window, watching the powdery flakes flutter in the dimming light, when my front door vibrated with a pounding fist.

Alarmed, I wondered who would stop by unannounced on such a snowy winter night. I opened the door to find a group of strangers grinning from ear to ear, their arms laden with boxes and bags.

Confused, but finding their joyous spirit contagious, I grinned right back. "Are you Susan?" The man stepped forward as he held out a box for me.

Nodding stupidly, unable to find my voice, I was sure they thought I was mentally deficient.

"These are for you." The woman thrust another box at me with a huge, beaming smile. The porch light and the snow falling behind her cast a glow over her dark hair, lending her an angelic appearance.

I looked down into her box. It was filled to the top with delicious treats, a fat turkey, and all the makings of a traditional Christmas dinner. My eyes filled with tears as the realization of why they were there washed over me.

Finally coming to my senses, I found my voice and invited them in. Following the husband were two children, staggering with the weight of their packages. The family introduced themselves to me and told me their packages were all gifts for my little family. This wonderful, beautiful family, who were total strangers to me, somehow knew exactly what we needed. They brought wrapped gifts for each of us, a full buffet for me to make on Christmas Day, and many "extras" that I could never afford. Visions of a beautiful, "normal" Christmas literally danced in my head. Somehow my secret wish for Christmas was materializing right in front of me. The desperate prayers of a single mom had been heard, and I knew right then that God had sent his angels my way.

My mysterious angels then handed me a white envelope, gave me another round of grins, and took turns hugging me. They wished me a Merry Christmas and disappeared into the night as suddenly as they had appeared.

Amazed and deeply touched, I looked around me at the boxes and gifts strewn at my feet and felt the ache of depression suddenly being transformed

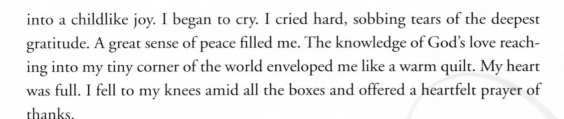

into a childlike joy. I began to cry. I cried hard, sobbing tears of the deepest gratitude. A great sense of peace filled me. The knowledge of God's love reaching into my tiny corner of the world enveloped me like a warm quilt. My heart was full. I fell to my knees amid all the boxes and offered a heartfelt prayer of thanks.

Getting to my feet, I wrapped myself in my blanket and sat once again to gaze out the window at the gently falling snow. Suddenly I remembered the envelope. Like a child I ripped it open and gasped at what I saw. A shower of bills flitted to the floor. Gathering them up, I began to count the five, ten, and twenty-dollar bills. As my vision blurred with tears, I counted the money, then counted it again to make sure I had it right. Sobbing again, I said it out loud: "One hundred dollars."

I looked at my children sleeping soundly, and through my tears I smiled my first happy, free-of-worry smile in a long, long time. My smile turned into a grin as I thought about tomorrow: Christmas Eve. One visit from complete strangers had magically turned a painful day into a special one that we would always remember... with happiness.

It is now several years since our Christmas angels visited. I have remarried, and our household is happy and richly blessed. Every year since that Christmas in 1993, we have chosen a family less blessed than we are. We bring them carefully selected gifts, food and treats, and as much money as we can spare. It's our way of passing on what was given to us. It's the "ripple effect" in motion. We hope that the cycle continues and that, someday, the families we share with will be able to pass it on, too.

BY SUSAN FAHNCKE

The Grab Bag

♥ ♥ ♥

FOR SOME REASON, my 12-year-old daughter, Jill, did not want to participate in her school grab bag. Getting her to choose something at the church craft sale took more energy than I had. No matter what I pointed to, she turned up her nose.

"I'm not going to school that day, and that's final!" she insisted. I hadn't seen her stomp her foot in a while, and doing it in our church basement was a true test of my patience.

"Jill, I don't understand why you're being so obstinate over this."

"You don't have to understand. Just leave me alone!" And with that, she ran out of the church basement clutching her jacket.

I finished my own shopping and went out to my car. She was leaning against it, scowling.

I was tempted to not unlock her car door and just drive off. I was a seasoned veteran when it came to doing battle with my temperamental child. But it was cold enough that her toes would be blue by the time she walked home, and her fingertips would need to be held under warm water.

Jill slunk into the passenger seat and let out an extended sigh.

"Either tell me what's going on," I said, "or we're going to be discussing how long you'll be grounded."

"Grounded?"

I actually jumped at the pitch of her voice. I gave her my best I'm-in-no-mood-for-this! look, then put the car in gear and pulled out.

She blurted out one sentence. "Do you know how many kids can't afford to buy grab bag gifts?"

"Jill, I know you can afford a $5 gift. I don't want to hear..."

She interrupted me. "I can afford the gift; I'm not talking about me. I'm talking about the kids who come from the west side, the kids who come from the projects, the kids whose dads don't live at home anymore. *Those* kids. Do you know how embarrassed they are if they don't bring anything?"

"Why haven't you mentioned this before?"

"Would you have cared?"

"Jill, I think you know I would."

"Last year I got a half-empty bag of bubble bath. Everyone saw Mary Elizabeth put it in the Santa sack, everyone snickered when I opened it. Mary Elizabeth blushed all over, and the teacher didn't do anything."

Jill was pretty worked up, which I passed off as preteen angst.

"Look, Jill, I admire your...compassion. But hollering at me and making a scene in the church basement won't change the school grab bag. So, you tell me what will."

Aha, I thought. Something for her to stew over.

"I think it should be canceled," she said. "And I think you should call the school and make them do it."

"Why me?" I asked. "Why not you?"

"They aren't going to listen to me. I'm a kid. They'll listen to you. You're in the PTA. You're a homeroom mom. Everyone listens to you."

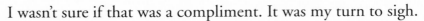

I wasn't sure if that was a compliment. It was my turn to sigh.

"Jill, I'll do it," I said. "But I want you to come up with an alternative. After that, I'll make an appointment with Ms. McAfee."

In my heart, I didn't want to call the principal, and I hoped Jill would drop it. Maybe tomorrow she'd be in a better mood.

No such luck. At breakfast before we left for church, Jill offered a plan. Instead of a grab bag, kids would drop whatever they could into the Santa sack, and Dad would dress up like Santa and take it to the homeless shelter."

"*Who's* going to dress up like Santa?" my husband asked over his cereal.

"You'd be a great Santa," Jill said, smiling that little smile she used to get her father to do what she wanted.

"That's a great idea," I chimed in, using the smile I'd learned to use to get him to do what *I* wanted.

And so began an annual event at Harwood Elementary. Chalk it up to pre-teen angst, chalk it up to compassion, or chalk it up to the holiday spirit, but Jill had made a difference. She worked hard, she encouraged her classmates to work hard, and she got as many people involved as she could.

The first year, we used the school van to transport the Santa sack. The following year, my husband used the van as well as our station wagon. This year, the school bus company donated a bus so that Santa could carry all the presents to the shelter.

Occasionally, Jill will overreact to some small annoyance, or pitch a fit when I least expect it, but she's a girl who can make a difference. And I'm very proud of her for that.

BY VALORIE NANCE

Mittens of Faith

❧   ❧   ❧

*T*HE BIBLE SAYS that "faith comes by hearing," but as a young girl in Depression-era Michigan, sometimes my faith came by watching.

On one cold December day, my mother answered the door and found a kind neighbor holding out a huge wool shawl. She handed it to Mom and said, "This is too large to be of much use to me, so I thought you could take it apart and use the yarn to make something for your children."

Raising five young children while her husband could find only part-time work weighed heavily on my young mother—especially with Christmas approaching. The shawl was an answer to her prayers.

Mom knew how to crochet but had never learned how to knit. The two were similar, so—as she unraveled the shawl into balls of yarn—she prayed for the ability to knit. She would teach herself.

With no money for knitting needles, Mom took the ribs from an old, broken umbrella and turned them into makeshift needles. Next, she took one of my father's socks apart, carefully examining the rows of stitching. She figured the stitches would have to go back together the same way they came out.

Soon she unraveled the mysteries of the craft, and after we'd all gone to bed she began knitting. The shawl furnished enough yarn for mittens for our whole family—a gift for each one of us. None were perfect, but each was a wondrous present on Christmas morning.

Many Christmases have come and gone and the mittens have long departed, but Mom's infinite example of faith remains in my heart. It is the best gift she ever gave me.

By Hilda Cheeseman

Oh Holy Night

Oh holy night!
The stars are brightly shining
It is the night of the dear Savior's birth!
Long lay the world in sin and error pining
Till he appear'd and the soul felt its worth.
A thrill of hope the weary world rejoices
For yonder breaks a new and glorious morn!

Fall on your knees
Oh hear the angel voices
Oh night divine
Oh night when Christ was born
Oh night divine
Oh night divine

J. S. Dwight, A. C. Adams

The Minister's Christmas Eve

🍃 🍃 🍃

REVEREND JOHN STONE SAT alone in the pew. Alone with his memories of Ethel Bledsoe…"Doc" Patterson…Hattie Whitlock…the ones who had died this year.

He smiled, remembering them fondly. Especially Hattie. Eighty years old. Heart of gold. Hearty laugh. Twinkling eyes always hinting at mischiefs she'd enjoyed.

Ethel…"Doc"…Hattie. What wonderful friends they'd been.…

John sat in the quiet of the church late in the day of Christmas Eve. Soon the pews would fill with the living. Sweet music and joyful voices would fill the air, and waiting hearts would lay like mangers ready for Christ. Soon the miracle would come, filling them briefly with its awe…only to become dormant for another year. Such, alas, was human nature.

All was ready. Garlands. Pine scent. Poinsettia. Candles waiting to be lit. Communion trays draped in linen. Beside the altar, the towering Norwegian pine glistened with tinsel and ornaments.

Tonight the children would gather around to open presents bearing their names. Last week they'd drawn names from a fish bowl. Each then bought a gift—a gift to cost less than five dollars—to wrap and place beneath the tree.

John heard from behind him the *swish, swish, swish* of a woman walking. Turning, he saw her and smiled.

"Hello, Alice."

"Hi, sweetheart." Sliding into the pew, Alice nestled beside him, resting her head on his shoulder. "Looks nice, doesn't it?" she said.

"Sure does. Absolutely beautiful...." Then, after a pause, he added, "Thanks for all your help."

"Of course, dear. You know I love it." Alice sighed.

"Tired, huh?"

Alice nodded. "Uh-huh...a little. You coming home with me?"

"No," John replied, glancing at his watch. Almost 5:00. "No...I think I'll go to the hospital...."

Alice saw the pain in John's eyes. She squeezed his hand tightly, hugged him, and whispered in his ear. "I love you."

She stood, letting go of John's hand. "See you later," she said. "I'm going home. Can't wait to climb into the tub."

"Enjoy."

John watched the woman he'd loved more and more through 20 years. He saw the loveliness of her. But, more, he saw the thankless hours she had spent making life a better place, a prettier place, a kinder and gentler place to be.

John returned to his study and put on his coat, gloves, and hat. He opened the door to the parking lot. In the darkness, through the streetlights, snowflakes fluttered. The air felt crisp. He breathed deeply, smelling woodsmoke from fireplaces. The wind bit at his cheeks. John scraped the snow from his windshield, started the car, and headed for All Children's Hospital.

Driving along, John felt the abundance of all he had: Alice. His work. Being alive....Then his mind wandered like sheep rambling in a pasture.

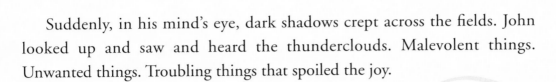

Suddenly, in his mind's eye, dark shadows crept across the fields. John looked up and saw and heard the thunderclouds. Malevolent things. Unwanted things. Troubling things that spoiled the joy.

His thoughts turned to little Gary Potter and Sally Jones—the children he was going to visit. They lay, sequestered from the season—the celebration of Christ's birth—dying in All Children's Hospital. Gary was dying from brain cancer; Sally from a defective heart.

Darker, more threatening, the thunderclouds boiled, filled with life's unfairnesses. Yes, this year had taken its toll. Ethel and "Doc" and Hattie. They had passed away, but they had died in their later years.

These two children were eight and nine years old! Why? What purpose served? What good is there in any of it? What good at all?

John pulled into the hospital parking lot. Shutting off the lights and ignition, he slumped over the steering wheel, feeling the duty to pray. But that's all it was—a sense of duty—like the duty felt by marching soldiers heading into battle. Given a choice, they'd turn around and go back home.

John raised his head from the steering wheel, then opened the door. Slamming it hard, he crunched his way, step by step, to the hospital's doors. Whatever prayers he might have said hung frozen in the night air.

Room 334. Sally's room. As John approached, he could feel the strain, the tension—like a storm-downed electrical line—sizzling, hissing, crackling, through the door. Laughs too big. Voices too loud. Smiles stretched tight like rubber bands. A room full of loved ones busy pretending....

"How're you doing?" Nodding heads. Tight-lipped smiles. Patting backs. Stiff hugs. Shaking hands. "OK." "OK." "OK."

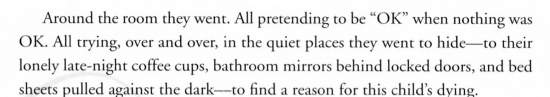

Around the room they went. All pretending to be "OK" when nothing was OK. All trying, over and over, in the quiet places they went to hide—to their lonely late-night coffee cups, bathroom mirrors behind locked doors, and bed sheets pulled against the dark—to find a reason for this child's dying.

No words. No signs. No nothing. So, they prayed and prayed and hoped and hoped and pretended and pretended, waiting for death. . . .

They clung to ageless euphemisms like life buoys flung to drowning sailors:

"The good die young. . . ."

"She'll be in a better place. . . ."

"God moves in mysterious ways. . . ."

Then, with pleading eyes, they'd look to Reverend Stone.

It was easy to deal with death when someone was old and death ended suffering. Or when a deformed baby died stillborn. But death, when it served no kind purpose, was sharp and cruel.

Feeding souls in times such as these was part of John's job.

John gestured Sally's father to come to the door. John asked, "How's she doing, Ed? Has the doctor been in yet?"

Ed nodded. "Dr. Jacoby was just here . . . just left." Ed took a deep breath, then sighed heavily. "Not good news. They've done all they can. Her heart's just runnin' outta steam, Reverend. She's got, maybe, a week to live . . . a week, at most. If we don't have a miracle . . . a transplant . . . by then, well, you know, she's . . ." His voice quivered. "She's . . . she's just dead. . . ."

"Oh, Ed, I'm so sorry. . . . Is there anything, *anything,* I can do?"

"No. I don't think so. Not right now. Thanks, though. Thanks for askin'. An' thanks for bein' here. It means a lot. It really does."

Ed turned and walked back into the room. John watched, feeling the tonnage on Ed's weary, stooped shoulders.

John took the elevator to the sixth floor. Gary Potter's room. Same song, different verse. The bad news—only a few days to live. The good news—little if any pain.

John sat for a while at Gary's side, talking of the rod and reel Gary wanted for Christmas and of how they'd go fishing together next spring after Gary got out of the hospital. Then in the hall, John consoled Bill and Wanda, Gary's parents. They asked him to pray. He held their hands and he did. He left the hospital with a heavy heart....

The church was abuzz with the magic of Christmas. The pews swelled full of starched white shirts and colorful sweaters and woolen dresses and jewels and furs and high-heeled shoes. Greetings and laughter and sundry sounds of restless children filled the air.

Then came the organ, the choir, the singing, the joyous singing. "Joy to the world, the Lord has come...." All eyes focused on John, with his black robe billowing, Bible in hand, and the service began.

John kept the sermon brief. The children, like tethered colts, could dash from their seats to the Christmas tree and their long-awaited presents.

John nodded his head. From the back of the church came the jingling of bells and a hearty *"Ho...ho...ho!"* All dressed in red came pudgy, red-cheeked Ernie Sickles, looking every bit like Santa Claus.

Ernie led the children to the tree, then, one by one, he passed out the gifts. The church was a flurry of bows and ribbons and wrapping paper as the children tore into their packages. Eventually, the frenzy subsided.

It looked like all the gifts had been opened, but up in the branches, almost hidden from view, was a large red envelope. Ernie stretched and reached, pulling it from the branches.

He cocked his head quizzically. Not knowing for sure what to do, he walked across the sanctuary, handing the envelope to John. John gazed at the words on the envelope: "From Gary, To Sally."

John looked up, his eyes sweeping the congregation. They landed on Shirley, Gary Potter's mother. John's eyes asked, "Shall I open it?" Shirley nodded yes.

John cleared his throat, then announced to the congregation, "This is a gift from Gary Potter to Sally Jones." With that the congregation, even the children, grew silent. They knew this would be the last Christmas for Gary and Sally. At once they felt the sadness of it.

Carefully, John sliced the envelope open. He pulled out a folded piece of blue construction paper. He looked at the picture—and read the words to himself. Tears welled, then rolled from his eyes, trickling down his cheeks. His throat swelled shut. For a moment he couldn't speak. All he could do was look at the faces waiting for him to speak.

Holding up the picture, John stammered: "This is an angel. See his white robe? See his sparkly, glittered wings? See his smile . . . his golden halo?"

In silence, the congregation nodded.

"And here, below it, are printed these words: 'I give my heart to Sally.'"

Gary died three days later. Sally's transplant was a success.

BY LARRY E. SCOTT

The Receipt

❦ ❦ ❦

I FOUND IT WHEN I was going through my father's files. Somehow sticking a store receipt in among my husband's medical records seemed out of character for Dad. It wasn't that my father hadn't saved other surprising things. He had. I'd found my report cards, thank you notes my children had written him, and warranties for all the appliances my folks had ever owned. When he left his medical practice, he brought our files home. Everything had been carefully filed and lovingly labeled. Undoubtedly, there had been a reason why Dad dropped this particular receipt into my husband Frank's file.

Though unwrinkled, the receipt was old, dated December 3, 1984. What possible reason could my father have had for saving it? A word was written in the center of the receipt, in my father's physician handwriting. The word appeared to be "gift." The price listed for the gift was $67.50, plus tax, and the shipping address was to my father's office in New Jersey. Why had he mailed a gift to himself? The name of the store where the gift had been purchased seemed familiar, but I couldn't quite place it. I laid the receipt aside and continued sorting through his sturdy, old oak desk with tears in my eyes.

I found a carbon of a letter Dad had written Frank shortly before our marriage. I smiled as I read his suggestion for a successful marriage as well as his closing words: "Take care of my little girl." I put the letter in the pile of papers to save.

I did throw away the copy of the letter Dad had written to the doctor who had performed Frank's knee surgery. Back then, knee problems weren't routinely corrected arthroscopically, and recuperation took several months. Frank, whose whole life had revolved around active sports, had been faced with finding a more sedentary hobby. The shop teacher from the school where he coached suggested wood carving. Our son, Mike, used all of his Christmas money to buy his dad carving knives, so Frank wanted to at least try them.

His first bird looked like a battleship, but because he couldn't pitch softball that summer, he kept carving. By fall he had four decoys finished . . . ducks that didn't look too bad. He gave all four away for Christmas presents to relatives.

Mike kindly suggested that he try selling some. Since Frank couldn't play city-league basketball, he took Mike seriously.

By spring Frank had finished two more decoys. He took them to a shop in the mall. The owner, Ann, said she'd take the two decoys on consignment and add a 35-percent commission to the price he wanted to get for them.

The ducks sat in the shop throughout the summer. They sat through September. In November the owner tied red bows around their necks and even set one in the window. We checked on it each time we went to the mall. Neither duck sold in November. I remember writing to my folks to tell them how discouraged Frank got after our trips to the mall. Mom wrote back saying she was sure he'd sell one soon. And he did! Shortly before Christmas,

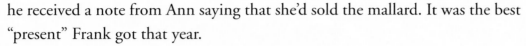

he received a note from Ann saying that she'd sold the mallard. It was the best "present" Frank got that year.

He was so pleased and excited. That sale gave him the confidence to keep on carving, and his work continued to improve. Dad had even saved a pristine copy of the gallery publicity fliers. He was proud of Frank's growing reputation as a craftsman.

I whirled around on Dad's desk chair remembering how I had loved to spin on it when I was small, even though I risked a scolding. As I spun, I tried to remember the name of the shop where that first decoy had sold. The Olive Tree—that was the name! The Olive Tree was the name of the store on the unexplained receipt. Dad must have bought the decoy and had it shipped to himself.

But why did he buy it? Frank would have given it to him, or if Dad had insisted on paying, he'd have sold it to him without the commission.

My eyes welled with tears as I realized that Dad had given Frank a gift—a gift of encouragement. The receipt was now a gift to me. It was as though my father was sharing one more Christmas message. Dad wanted to show me the power of such a gift and encourage me to find ways to give similar gifts to others.

BY ELLEN JAVERNICK

The only real blind person at Christmastime is he who has not Christmas in his heart.

HELEN KELLER (1880–1968)

Gift-wrapped

❧ ❧ ❧

RED RIBBON STRETCHED its arms wide. Dangling from the large bow was a hand-stenciled tag bearing the names of the room's occupants. The door looked like a giant present, wrapped especially for Christmas.

"It's just not enough," Rosa sighed.

"What isn't enough?" asked Marta.

"The holiday decorations. They don't do much to brighten up the place, do they?" Rosa tore off another strip of masking tape and used it to anchor the gold and red swags.

"Oh, I don't know." Marta stepped back to observe their handiwork. "Pass me that plastic poinsettia. *Bueno.* Does that help?"

Hands on hips, Rosa surveyed the tinsel-draped hallway where identical doors boasted their festive handiwork.

"Honestly, Marta, I'm not sure what helps."

"You're talking about more than the decorations, aren't you?"

"Well, I love volunteering here," said Rosa, meaning Sierra Vista Manor, "but it's hard to watch the residents. They're so . . . housebound. They have so few personal choices." Rosa sighed. "It hurts to see these people stripped of their feelings of self-worth. I just wish I could help."

The two friends walked back to the receiving area. Several large cardboard boxes surrounded the front desk, and others spilled from the counter.

"Feliz Navidad!" greeted the receptionist.

"What are all these things?" asked Marta, pointing to the precarious piles.

"A big mistake, I think," the receptionist said. "A man came in saying his mother had lived here several years ago and he wanted to donate items for Christmas. Of course, I assumed they were gifts for the residents. But when I opened the boxes . . ."

"It's toys!" exclaimed Rosa. "All sorts of toys." She pawed through the contents of the largest container.

"What do you mean, toys?" Marta said. "Didn't he read the sign? This is a nursing home. What was he thinking?"

"He was thinking that these would be perfect," said Rosa. "And I think so, too." Rosa tore open box after box, smiling over soap bubbles, card games, and clay. Unpacking crayons, stickers, and books. Sorting through paint sets, puzzles, and checkers.

Using her foot, the receptionist scooted one last, large, but lightweight container toward Rosa.

"This came, too," she said.

Running a letter opener between the flaps, Rosa broke the seal.

"Wrapping paper? Gift bags? Tape? Scissors? Name tags?" Marta puzzled over each item as her friend lifted them from the tissue-lined box.

Rosa, though, nearly squealed in her excitement.

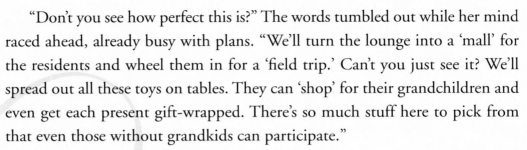

"Don't you see how perfect this is?" The words tumbled out while her mind raced ahead, already busy with plans. "We'll turn the lounge into a 'mall' for the residents and wheel them in for a 'field trip.' Can't you just see it? We'll spread out all these toys on tables. They can 'shop' for their grandchildren and even get each present gift-wrapped. There's so much stuff here to pick from that even those without grandkids can participate."

Marta's eyes twinkled with enthusiasm. "I know! Let's get a list of children's names from the local shelter. The residents can 'adopt' them and select toys for their new 'family.'"

She paused. "Who do you suppose donated these things, anyway?"

"An angel," Rosa said firmly. "Who else would remember that grandparents love their grandchildren? Who else would supply them with an opportunity to choose? Who else would restore their dignity in such a perfect way?"

"True," Marta agreed. "Who else would think to provide our grandmas and grandpas with the best gift of all—an opportunity to give?"

By Carol McAdoo Rehme

O Christmas tree, O Christmas tree,
Your leaves are faithful ever!
Not only green when summer glows
But in the winter when it snows.
O Christmas tree, O Christmas tree,
Your leaves are faithful ever!

A Wish for Eric

♥   ♥   ♥

$\mathcal{S}$OMETIMES, PARENTS DON'T always know best. When our ten-year-old son, Jordan, announced that he wanted a specific toy for Christmas, my husband, Jim, and I wondered if we could afford it. It was one of many things he had asked for, but he made it clear that this gift was something he *must* have. It was a boy's mountain bike, and a rather pricey one at that.

For days afterward, he hounded us about the bike, making sure we knew the exact model, size, and brand name. I reminded Jordan that his own bike was perfectly fine. Jordan would just scowl, then reiterate how critical it was that he got this bike for Christmas.

Naturally, Jim and I wondered if perhaps we had spoiled our son too much. We tried to instill lessons in Jordan's mind, lessons about greed and moderation and fiscal responsibility. He would sit there and listen, and then he would just say something like, "Well, then don't get me all that other stuff. Just make sure I get the bike."

Wow, I thought, this is pretty demanding behavior for a ten-year-old. Jim and I sat down that night with Jordan and told him the truth about life: that you can't always get what you want, that money doesn't grow on trees, and so on. Again, Jordan listened politely, then sighed and said all over again, "Then please don't buy me anything else for Christmas, or my birthday, or for Christmas next year even. Just get me the bike!"

Jim and I decided that we would have to talk to Jordan a little more firmly the following day. He was taking us for granted, and it was going to stop now.

The next afternoon Jordan came home from school, and I was about to confront him when I noticed he was on the telephone. I waited politely for him to finish, rehearsing what I would say, when I began to listen to him on the phone. He was trying to console someone on the other end of the phone, saying, "Don't worry, I'll get you the bike. . . . I want you to have the bike. . . . It will be OK; don't cry." I heard Jordan call the person Eric, and after Jordan hung up the phone, I stepped into the room.

"Who is Eric?" I asked firmly. Jordan got very quiet, but before he could answer, the phone rang again. This time I answered it, and it was a woman's voice I didn't recognize. She introduced herself as Helen Bradley, Eric's mother. She was calling to tell me what a wonderful son I had. As I listened, stunned and totally taken off guard, she explained to me that Eric was dying of an inoperable brain tumor, and that he had asked for a very expensive mountain bike for Christmas. Somehow, Eric had conveyed to Jordan that his family was not financially well off and could not afford the bike, and Jordan had taken it upon himself to get the bike for Eric.

I was speechless. Helen got very quiet as she told me that she appreciated our kindness and generosity, but that she and her

husband insisted that we not buy the bike. "Jordan is such an angel, you must be so proud," she said in a voice thick with emotion. "But please don't let him feel he must take on this burden. We will find a way to get the bike." We talked for a few moments more and then hung up. I looked at my son, who was standing there with his head hanging down sheepishly. All of the anger had left me. Without a word, I hugged him tightly.

When Jim came home, I told him what our son had done. He was so proud, so amazed. And so we decided to help Jordan, not by buying the bike ourselves, but by coming up with a wonderful plan for Jordan to raise the money himself. We held a garage sale a week later, and Jordan sold off enough of his old toys and clothes to pay for almost the entire bike. The rest would come out of his allowance, and three days later we went to Eric's house.

Helen was overcome with emotion when we told her how Jordan had acquired the money, earning it rather than asking us for it. She was almost as proud of him as we were, and we stood there together as Jordan presented the bike to Eric, and made a dying boy's wish come true.

By Marie Jones

Yes, Virginia, there is a Santa Claus. He exists as certainly as love and generosity and devotion exist.
Francis P. Church, *New York Sun*, September 21, 1897

Christmas Joy

❦ ❦ ❦

*I*F YOU'VE EVER STRUGGLED to start a new business, you can appreciate our family's financial situation during the Christmas season of 1960. My husband, Chester, had a fledgling appliance-repair service he was operating out of our home, and during the cold months of winter, there were, of course, no air conditioners to fix and only a few refrigerators needing attention. Business was sagging.

At that time, in addition to our own eight children, we had two families from out of town staying with us. The first family was that of a friend whose husband had died the previous year. She had come with her eight children from Stilwell, Oklahoma, hoping to find a job. The second family had arrived unexpectedly from California: Chester's brother, his wife, and their three children. They remained our guests while Chester's brother also looked for work. A total of 24 people were living together in our six-room home as Christmas drew near!

As the reality set in that we would have no money for presents—or even for a tree—we took the children aside and, holding back our tears, explained that we would be having a different kind of Christmas this year. We told them that although we would not be buying presents, they could make gifts for one another out of paper. Christmas dinner would also be unconventional: beans and cornbread. As we searched their faces for a response, they all agreed that this arrangement was OK with them. They liked beans, they said.

I prepared for the holiday as best I could. I made rag dolls for the small children, but I had nothing for the older ones. I used strips of newspaper and flour-and-water glue to fashion a papier-mâché nativity, which I painted and put on display.

Then, just before his winter break, our ten-year-old son Larry came home from school with some wonderful news. His home-room teacher had told him that on the last day of classes he could take home the Christmas tree that was stand-ing in the classroom. We were all thrilled and antici-pated the day when Larry would bring the tree home. But when the day arrived, Larry walked through the door empty-handed. He was met with stares of shock and disappointment.

"Larry! Where is the tree?" we all asked in uni-son. Larry explained that a boy in his class and his sister, whose father had died just a few days earlier, were not going to have a Christmas tree that year. Larry had given the tree to his classmate.

Hearing this, we were moved by what Larry had done, and we were proud of his generous spirit. Then, seizing the moment as an opportunity to teach the younger children, our oldest son, a 17-year-old, reminded them of how fortunate and blessed we all were to have one another, to have our health, to have love, and to have the nativity that Mom

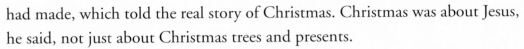

had made, which told the real story of Christmas. Christmas was about Jesus, he said, not just about Christmas trees and presents.

With this pep talk, the children got busy making paper stars and snowflakes. Ideas for gifts began to emerge. One of the girls asked if she could give Grandma a small bottle of toilet water she was saving for special occasions. She had only used it a couple times, she said.

Smiling, I said, "Of course! If it's from your heart, it's a wonderful present."

"It's snowing, Mama!" the children announced excitedly. They were looking out the kitchen window, and as I joined them to watch, I saw the beautiful, soft flakes falling noiselessly on the windowpane. Right then, I said a silent thank-you to God for a warm, dry home and the potato soup that was steaming on the stove. As I considered the Lord's goodness, I realized it was a miracle that the kettle had never run out of food, no matter how many people had eaten from it in the last two months.

Just then, the phone rang. "A-1 Appliance Repair," I answered. The woman's voice on the other end of the line gave the name of a business and wanted to know if Chester could come to the store's location. Then she continued, "Someone told me you were in an accident and broke your leg. How are you?"

I told her that although I had been in an accident the previous week, no one had been injured. "The truck that ran into me had no insurance, and our car was smashed up, but everyone was OK, thank God."

There was a long pause at the other end of the line before the woman said, "Oh! Well, we always make up a food box to help someone who is laid up or who needs it. We thought you were hurt and needed a little help." There was another pause. "Would we hurt your feelings if we offered it to you?"

I thanked her and told her that we would appreciate their gift. Then she asked, "Do you have your tree up yet?"

"No, we haven't."

"Well, we have a big one here. It would be a shame to leave it in an empty store over Christmas." She said we could take the tree and leave the decorations on it, as they did not have time to take them off. "We heard you have a big family of four or five children," she added.

"Yes, eight!" I said. "This is great! Just great! Thank you so much!" and I hung up the phone.

As Chester got into the pickup with our two oldest sons, I lamented, "I didn't even tell her Merry Christmas!" Chester assured me that he would tell her for me and then drove off. The children watched them leave and chattered among themselves about having a Christmas tree. Chester and the boys returned with the most beautiful tree I had ever seen.

"Look! Look! Mama, how pretty!" the children jumped up and down gleefully.

Following the tree came four big boxes of groceries and a huge turkey. One of the children noticed my reaction and said, "Mama, don't cry."

"I'm crying because I'm happy," I said, smiling through my tears.

The phone rang again. It was the same voice. I thanked her for everything, but she said she had forgotten to give Chester some door prizes that hadn't been claimed. Also, there was a box of clothing that the store next door wanted to give us. She asked to please send Chester right away if we would like to have them. She and the others at the store were ready to close up and go home for the holiday, but they would wait for us to come.

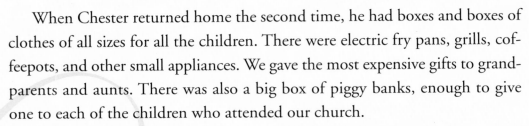

When Chester returned home the second time, he had boxes and boxes of clothes of all sizes for all the children. There were electric fry pans, grills, coffeepots, and other small appliances. We gave the most expensive gifts to grandparents and aunts. There was also a big box of piggy banks, enough to give one to each of the children who attended our church.

What a wonderful Christmas we had that lean year of 1960. The amazing thing to me is that we didn't even ask God for it, but he still provided. We certainly thanked him, though—thanked him for speaking softly to folks who could give, and who did give. They gave to a home that had 24 people in it, though the ones who gave did not know this until after Christmas when we told them.

We named our ninth and last child Joy, in remembrance of all the joy God has given us. We don't always think to pray for it, but we always remember to be grateful.

BY WILMA J. MASINGALE

When [the wise men] saw that the star had stopped, they were overwhelmed with joy. On entering the house, they saw the child with Mary his mother; and they knelt down and paid him homage.

MATTHEW 2:10–11

The Samaritan

❧   ❧   ❧

JOHN CHRISTOPHER STOOD there before the burning rubble that was once a single-family home and wondered why such a terrible thing would occur one day before Christmas Eve, the most holy of nights. He had been an insurance agent for years, and had seen a lot of tragic circumstances, but this was one of the most heartbreaking.

The house, a tiny urban dwelling in one of the city's most run-down neighborhoods, had caught fire from a gas leak. Luckily, the Parker family had made it out alive. They just sat in silence, staring at the smoking mess they had once called home. John went over to them and tried to console them. The parents were grateful for his kind words, but they were devastated at the loss of what little Christmas joy they had been preparing for their two small children.

John spoke with them for an hour, going over the meager insurance coverage they had been able to afford, and assuring them that he would do everything he could to get them the most money back so that they could rebuild their home. He knew they could never rebuild their dreams. The children, ages six and eight, were quiet. One of them, the little boy, clutched a teddy bear. John directed them to a Red Cross representative, who would set up the family at a local shelter.

As he watched them go, he wondered why these things often seemed to happen to the people who could least afford it. He knew that the insurance policy they had would not cover half of the expenses to rebuild, and very little of their personal property, yet it had been all they could afford. John felt his heart go heavy at the thought of what this family would face in the weeks and months ahead. He wondered if there was much he could do. He then realized that—although he might not be able to change their future—he could do something to change their tomorrow.

That night, as many of his colleagues were preparing to close up for the holiday vacation, John sat his staff down and told them about the fire and the poor Parker family that would not know Christmas this year. He didn't expect any of them to jump to his aid. After all, it was almost Christmas and they all had families and plans of their own.

But the outpouring of care and concern was more than John had hoped for. In a feverish rush of activity, every staff member present vowed to do something for the family, some even agreeing to postpone their travel plans for a few hours. John felt the heaviness in his heart lift as, all around him, evidence of real Christmas spirit made itself known. John's assistant, Andrea, volunteered to coordinate their actions, and everyone was off to do their part to make this a special holiday for the Parker family.

The next day, the staff came in one by one and deposited food, gifts, toys, and cookies. John had even brought a decorated miniature Christmas tree topped with a beautiful angel. The entire staff then donned Santa hats and drove in a caravan to the Red Cross shelter, where the family was staying.

With John in the lead, the band of angels descended upon the Parker family with a Christmas surprise no one at the shelter would ever forget. The children got toys and clothes, and cookies and punch were passed around to everyone, including the shelter volunteers. John smiled, his heart swelling with pride and happiness, as his colleagues led Christmas carols and Andrea recited "The Night Before Christmas." And right before nightfall, before the staff members had to leave to attend to their own families, they presented the Parker family with the beautiful Christmas tree.

John was the last to leave, but not before he was the recipient of some mighty big hugs and grateful, teary-eyed smiles. Mr. and Mrs. Parker blessed him, calling him their special angel. John blushed, but he was so glad they were able to smile amidst the loss they had suffered. As he drove home to his awaiting family, John knew he had done what he could for the Parkers, and somehow God would take care of the rest.

BY DAUPHINE JONES

May the fire of this log warm the cold; may the hungry be fed; may the weary find rest, and may all enjoy Heaven's peace.

TRADITIONAL PRAYER SAID WHEN YULE LOG IS LIT

The Gift

"ARE YOU SURE YOU WANT to do this, Mom?" I cradle the phone receiver against my shoulder while using my hands to button my four-year-old daughter's pajama shirt. "It can wait."

"No. It has to be tonight, Christmas Eve," Mom firmly insists. "Your brother's condition is fading. I need to do this while he's still alive. So please, Robyn, don't try to make sense out of my request. You and Auntie gather up his Christmas gifts and bring them to the hospital."

I hang up the phone. Arguing with a woman who is about to lose a child is senseless. Due to a sudden brain aneurysm, my brother is in a coma from which there is no chance of recovery. The rest of our family accepted this sad fact several days ago, but only now is Mom ready to let Samuel go. My brother is 27, but he is still as much her baby today as he was the day he was born.

"What's wrong?" Auntie sits in the rocking chair, my three-month-old daughter cradled in her loving arms. "Was that your mother? Is Samuel worse?"

Auntie is not blood-related, but for as long as I can remember she's been a loved member of our entire Brooklyn neighborhood. Auntie, 80 years old, is what is termed simpleminded, but there is nothing simple about her when it comes to compassion. She's always the first to come to a neighbor's aid. As soon as word of my brother's collapse reached Auntie, she moved in with my widowed mother to help her until I could manage to get here from my out-of-state home.

The expression on my face tells Auntie what she needs to know. Tears glisten in her blue eyes, but she blinks them away. If strength is what my mother needs this night, then it will be strength this petite woman will give to her friend.

We decide my husband will stay with our two daughters while Auntie and I, with brightly wrapped gifts carefully placed in three large shopping bags, will go to the hospital. Despite the cheery holiday decorations, a hospital on Christmas Eve is a somber place. Everyone there, staff included, would rather be home with family and friends.

Mom is waiting for us in the visitors' lounge. I'm glad. My brother's hospital roommate makes me nervous. It's not as if he's ever said or done anything to me. He doesn't even acknowledge me when I say hello. I know his name is Joe, but the nurses have told me he's a former gang member who spent the majority of his life in prison. A thin curtain is all that separates my brother's bed from Joe's, and occasionally I'll get a quick look at him.

Joe is an immense man, his hard muscles rippling plainly beneath the fabric of his hospital gown. His wide shoulders display a variety of tattoos, and there are scars across the right side of his shaved head. Big brown eyes, set in a round face the color of creamed coffee, are in constant motion. Everyone, other then those who must tend to him, avoids him. Joe's sarcasm is biting and his mannerisms intimidating.

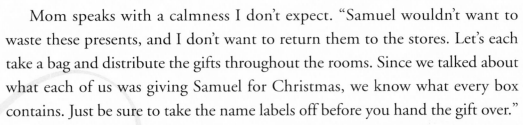

Mom speaks with a calmness I don't expect. "Samuel wouldn't want to waste these presents, and I don't want to return them to the stores. Let's each take a bag and distribute the gifts throughout the rooms. Since we talked about what each of us was giving Samuel for Christmas, we know what every box contains. Just be sure to take the name labels off before you hand the gift over."

I admire my mother's bravery. Now that I am a mother myself, I understand the powerful love a woman feels for her children. Yet, despite the heartbreaking loss my mother will soon face, she is determined to bring a bit of cheer to others.

I finish first and wait in the hallway for Auntie and Mom. I see Auntie coming from my brother's room. She looks quite like Mrs. Santa Claus in her ankle-length red velvet skirt, green wool sweater, and plaid shawl draped over her tiny shoulders. There's even a sprig of mistletoe one of the nurses tucked into her silver hair.

"I'm done," she happily announces. "I just gave the last package, the one in the rectangle box, to Joe."

"Oh Auntie . . . not that one." My face flushes with humiliation, then anger at myself for snapping at her. It was my elder daughter's present for her uncle, and I should have made sure I was the one to give it to another patient. "It's all right, Auntie. Go find Mom. Make sure she has something to eat. I'll be along in a few minutes."

I'm too late to stop Joe from opening the package. Green wrapping paper and red bows lie on the flat blanket where Joe's two legs, amputated last week, should be. In his hands he holds the gray bedroom slippers that Auntie just gave to him.

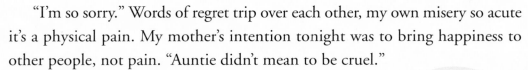

"I'm so sorry." Words of regret trip over each other, my own misery so acute it's a physical pain. My mother's intention tonight was to bring happiness to other people, not pain. "Auntie didn't mean to be cruel."

"Nobody's given me a present in 20 years. I guess I just wasn't worth nothing to nobody. So it don't matter that I don't have feet to put the slippers on." Joe gulps hard, and a steady stream of tears begin to slip down his face. "I'm so happy your auntie thought me deserving." He cradles the slippers to him as if they are a living, breathing being.

I don't reply. No words need to be said. Instead I go to the other side of the curtain and sit by my dying brother's side. I too am crying, but not for the life soon to be lost. No. My tears flow for Joe, and the joy he received from the mistaken present.

Thomas died on December 27. I don't know what happened to Joe. However, I will always remember the lesson I learned that Christmas Eve of 1977: The true spirit of Christmas is not contained in a physical gift; it is contained in the heart.

By Jackie Clements-Marenda

Save a branch of your Christmas tree and use it to start the New Year's fire.

Anne Wall Frank

A Perfect Present

❦   ❦   ❦

"DARLIN', GET YOUR MOMMA some ice, please." I took her glass and did a little curtsy. That always made her smile after she had a drink or two. We were the first family on our block to get a refrigerator with an ice dispenser in the door, and it only took a moment to fill her glass.

"You are a lovely child!" she said when I handed her the glass. "I'm awfully thirsty so I'll just drink this, then I'm going to rest a while. Be a dear and answer the phone if it rings so it doesn't wake me."

I nodded and looked just for an instant at the pool in our backyard. I knew that meant I had to stay inside until she woke up, and I was disappointed.

"Come upstairs with me, Charlotte, I want to show you something."

I went mostly to make sure she didn't trip on the stairs. We walked into her darkened bedroom and she sat on the edge of the bed, having already forgotten whatever it was she wanted to show me. I pulled off her gold mule slippers and helped her get her legs up on the bed. She was asleep almost immediately, so I went back and grabbed the glass, pouring ice and amber liquid into the bathroom sink.

I went downstairs to wake Lilli, my ten-year-old sister. Sometimes Lilli was even harder to rouse than Momma. I gave up and flopped into the La-Z-Boy in front of our big-screen TV.

The phone rang and I answered before it could ring again. It was our neighbor, Mrs. Hobbs, who wanted Momma's recipe for Christmas pudding cake, but I sure didn't know where to find it. I told her Momma would call her back.

That woke Lilli, who joined me on the recliner, resting her tousled head on my shoulder. "Lilli, wouldn't you like to swim in the pool today?"

"No."

"Come on, Lilli. It's November, so it isn't going to be warm enough to splash around out there much longer. Even Savannah, Georgia, gets cold come December."

Lilli didn't move. Her thumb slipped into her mouth, and I gently disengaged it. In all my 13 years, I'd never seen a sadder child.

I changed the subject. "Lilli, what do you want for Christmas?"

"Nothing." Lilli yawned and closed her eyes.

"Well, I do, and I want you to want it with me. If we both ask for the same thing, maybe we'll get it."

Lilli's interest wasn't piqued. She curled up closer. "What are you gonna ask for? We already have everything."

"We'll tell Momma that we don't need any presents; we just want her to stop drinking. That would be the best present of all." I looked intently at Lilli's face to see her reaction. She looked frightened, which surprised me.

"No, Charlotte, let's not tell her that. She'll be mad, or hurt, and it'll ruin Christmas."

"But Lilli, if she does quit, all of our Christmases to come will be so much better. We just have to make it through this one. Aunt Nancy says we can

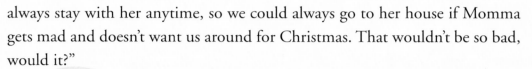

always stay with her anytime, so we could always go to her house if Momma gets mad and doesn't want us around for Christmas. That wouldn't be so bad, would it?"

Lilli eased out of our seat and put her thumb back in her mouth. "I'm going to watch TV in my room," she said. I heard her door close and her "Do Not Disturb" sign swinging on the doorknob.

Undaunted, I got out my school notebook and began composing my letter. The phone rang again, and I told him, "No, sir, I am not the lady of the house, but we still don't want any aluminum siding." I went back to my desk and started over.

Lilli was asleep when Momma got up. "Hi, Momma. Did you have a good rest?"

"You know I did, Sugar. Did I get any calls?"

"Yes, ma'am. Mrs. Hobbs called for your Christmas pudding cake recipe."

"Oh, that woman. I have to give her that recipe every year. What does she do with it—gobble it up with the cake?" Momma grinned and shuffled into the kitchen.

I put my notebook in my desk and followed her to the kitchen. "Want to go out and play in the pool with me?" I asked, trying to sound really enthusiastic.

"Now, Charlotte, you know I don't go in the water the day after I've had my hair done."

"It's been three days, Momma, and I promise I won't splash. You can just sit on the edge of the pool while I show you how good I'm getting at the backstroke."

"Three days already? I swear it seems like just yesterday I was at the salon. You go ahead without me, and I'll be out in a bit, Charlotte. I need to write that recipe before I forget."

I made as much noise as I could putting on my bathing suit, hoping Lilli would wake up and join me. I rolled the solar cover off the pool and inched down the steps into the water. I practiced my backstroke and holding my breath underwater. Then I tried diving into the deep end. Neither Momma nor Lilli joined me, so I finally grabbed the towel I'd laid next to Momma's deck chair and went in to see what they were doing.

I slid the patio door closed, and the cool air conditioning raised goose bumps on my arms. "Momma," I called, but she didn't answer. I went into the den, and there she was, sitting at my desk, reading my notebook. I sucked a deep breath and stood there, still as a statue.

Momma never looked up. She just started reading aloud.

"Dear Momma. This year for Christmas, Lilli and I would like to ask you for a very special gift. We love you so much that we want to share our present with you." Momma's voice was shaking. Lilli slid in behind me and draped my arm around her neck. Momma just continued to read.

"We would be so happy if you would stop drinking and throw away all the bottles of spirits that you have." I used "spirits" on my second version because I thought it sounded more genteel than "gin." Momma always prided herself on being a genteel Southern woman.

"We think it would be awesome to spend Christmas week together, if you wouldn't drink anything as your present to us. We love you, and..." The letter stopped there because I hadn't finished it. Momma read it again, this time louder. Lilli trembled, but Momma's voice was no longer shaking. I could tell she was angry, and my first thought was to get her a drink—maybe even a "double."

I watched as my notebook flew through the air, smacking the television screen and flopping onto the Persian rug. It was silent except for the sound of Lilli sucking her thumb. Momma covered her face with her hands, then patted her French twist to make sure every hair was in place. She turned to us and asked what we wanted for dinner. She thought having a pizza delivered would be lovely. And though we didn't answer, she picked up the phone and hit the speed-dial number.

As she passed us, she patted my head and said, "I will take your Christmas wish under consideration." Not another word was said until she answered the door for the pizza driver. We got a free two-liter bottle of cola with our delivery, and all three of us drank it with our pizza.

The next day we had school, so Lilli and I went to our rooms early to lay out clothes and put our homework in our backpacks. I slipped into the den and retrieved my notebook. I was pretty sure I could hear Momma crying in her room, but I hurried by and went to bed.

Momma drove us to school in the morning and kissed us goodbye. I could see her convertible ease down the driveway. My stomach was in knots, and Lilli had her thumb in her mouth. I snatched it away, gave her a hug, and whispered "don't worry" before she scooted down the hall.

When Momma picked us up at three o'clock, she seemed perfectly steady, but sad. I chattered all the way home, trying to make it the happiest day we'd ever had, but I failed.

That was pretty much the pattern for the next couple weeks. Momma didn't drink, Lilli didn't talk, and I tried to put the best face on everything.

Then, before we went to church on Christmas Eve, Momma sat in front of the tree and had me take a picture of her—then another one "just in case." When she got up, she took my hand and grabbed Lilli's. "I am doing my very best to give you your Christmas wish," she said. "This isn't easy for me, but I've been going to meetings after I drop you at school, and that helps. I've thrown away all the . . . spirits in the house, and with your help—and God's— I think I can do this."

Lilli hugged Momma. I stood on tiptoes and gave her a kiss—one that wouldn't smear her makeup—and held onto both of them. I didn't want to let go. None of us did.

BY ELIZABETH TOOLE

Somehow not only for Christmas
But all the long year through,
The joy that you give to others
Is the joy that comes back to you.
And the more you spend in blessing
The poor and lonely and sad,
The more of your heart's possessing
Returns to make you glad.
JOHN GREENLEAF WHITTIER, "THE JOY OF GIVING"

Skip the Gifts

❦ ❦ ❦

"So, WHAT DO YOU WANT for Christmas this year?" Mike asked for possibly the thousandth time in the last few weeks.

Jane shrugged. Looking around, she surveyed their home, filled to capacity with a lifetime of mementos and treasured belongings. What else could they use, either one of them? She really couldn't think of a thing she needed or seriously wanted. Not that they were fabulously wealthy or anything like that. They were comfortable, settled nicely, not lacking anything major.

"Not a thing," she told her husband of 35 years. Studying their lovely home, she thought of Christmases past, years when their home bulged at the sides with family and friends, years when the kids were younger and eager to unwrap heaps of gaily wrapped presents. Her memories flooded her heart. So many wonderful years. So many great Christmases.

Their children were now grown, and this year their families were caught up in especially tight schedules. They'd stay in touch, of course, but they wouldn't be able to come for Christmas.

Jane didn't really mind. It was nice in some ways to have just the two of them again, the way it was at the very start of their life together.

"Can't think of anything?" Mike asked her yet again.

"How about you?" she responded, the start of an idea forming in the back of her mind.

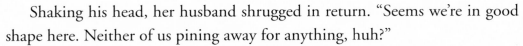

Shaking his head, her husband shrugged in return. "Seems we're in good shape here. Neither of us pining away for anything, huh?"

Then the appeal they'd been hearing for several days flashed across the TV again. Homeless families huddled together at the entrance to a shelter, their hands stuffed deep into shabby coat pockets, their faces red with cold, their heads bare.

The idea rushed through her mind as Jane watched the television screen. Her gaze met her husband's.

"We could skip gifts to one another this year," Mike suggested.

"We could use the money instead to help others," Jane finished. Both smiled, the matter settled between them. They had already selected gifts for the kids and grandkids. They had already found perfect items for friends and neighbors. But here was something that really needed doing, something they could do together that would make a difference.

They set to work immediately, pulling on their coats, heading for the nearest stores, searching out the warmest gloves, hats, and scarves they could find. Once home, Jane even dragged out all her balls of yarn left over from craft projects and crocheted as many tiny hats as she could, thinking of those children clinging to their parents for warmth.

As they worked gathering warm clothing for the homeless shelter, Mike heard an appeal on the radio for the Humane Society, which needed extra

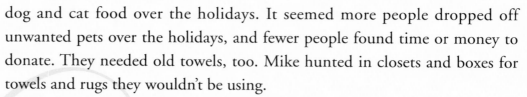

dog and cat food over the holidays. It seemed more people dropped off unwanted pets over the holidays, and fewer people found time or money to donate. They needed old towels, too. Mike hunted in closets and boxes for towels and rugs they wouldn't be using.

Jane hummed Christmas songs as she crocheted warm, colorful, tiny hats, adding pompons on top for fun, thinking of the comfort the little hats would bring. Meanwhile, Mike headed for the grocery store to buy sacks of dog and cat food.

When an announcement came over the radio about extra food needed for the food bank during the holiday season, Jane looked at Mike and he grinned back at her.

"Why not?" he asked.

She grinned in return. Why not? Jane scoured the grocery ads, searching for specials, stretching every dollar for the most food value. She found canned hams on special at one store and bought a dozen. Canned tuna showed up in another ad, and she brought home a bagful.

"We're starting to look like a warehouse," Jane told her husband.

"Not for long," he answered, busily sorting and stacking sacks of food. Christmas music played in the background, and both felt more energized about the holidays than ever before.

Bundled up in their oldest work clothes, they loaded the car and set off on deliveries. At the homeless shelter, a fellow glanced up at their ragged clothes and started to send them around to join the line of families waiting to get in. Mike laughed at the mistake. "No, we're here to bring donations," he explained as he led the way to their heavily laden car.

Jane felt her heart lift as one homeless man bent to help lift loaded bags from the backseat and eagerly tried on a brightly striped, hand-crocheted hat. Pulling the hat she'd made down over his cold-reddened ears, the man seemed to Jane suddenly years younger, lighter, more full of hope than he'd been moments before.

Jane and Mike were greeted with grateful delight at the Humane Society, where helpers rushed to unload sacks of food and towels and rugs. They could hear the yapping of pets discarded by their owners; those dogs would eat well until new homes were found.

At the food bank, eager hands lifted boxes of hams and tuna, peanut butter and soup. Poor children would have enough to eat because of their efforts.

At last, happily worn out, Jane and Mike returned home to their own comfortable house, their own Christmas decorations, their own gifts sent by family and friends. They had undoubtedly spent more than they'd originally intended, but both felt such an incredible sense of peace and joy that they couldn't begrudge a single cent.

Thinking of the homeless man with her striped hat over his cold ears, Jane smiled at her husband. "Best gift I ever gave," she told him, and both knew they'd found a perfect new tradition for their holidays.

By Karen M. Leet

The Christmas Truck

❦ ❦ ❦

WHEN YOU THINK no one believes in you, it's hard to believe in yourself. Kevin Anson, a handsome, young minister and single dad raising three children in Michigan, would be the first to agree with that statement.

Kevin's childhood was spent in a household dominated by a distant and disapproving stepfather. His stepdad was a college professor who never said a kind word to the boy. Although he was careful not to criticize Kevin too severely in front of his mother, whenever she wasn't around, the stepfather made a point of telling Kevin he would never amount to anything. "You're too stupid to go to college," he would say. "Don't even think of trying."

Kevin quickly lost interest in studying. As high school graduation approached, his mother urged him to enroll in the local community college, but Kevin kept putting it off. Meanwhile, his stepfather was pressuring him to leave. "It's high time you supported yourself," he snapped. Kevin agreed. He couldn't endure his stepfather's ill-concealed hostility much longer, so he found a job as a cashier in a supermarket and moved out on his own.

Life in the outside world is anything but friendly to a teenager with no experience, fending for himself. It's hardly surprising that Kevin felt lonely and insecure on his own. Soon he began looking for companionship.

Jenny was a dark-haired, blue-eyed beauty three years younger than Kevin. A junior-high dropout from a broken family, she'd been moving from one boyfriend's house to another in order to support herself. Jenny was a great deal more street savvy than Kevin, and she used her flirtatious charms to get whatever she needed—food, clothing, or a place to stay. She was a troubled soul, but Kevin didn't see that. He saw a bubbly, fun-loving girl who seemed to be fascinated with him.

Soon Jenny moved into Kevin's apartment. She introduced him to a host of friends, all streetwise young people like herself, who never held jobs for very long but somehow managed to keep a supply of drugs and alcohol on hand. When they partied late into the night and Kevin found it difficult to get up for work, Jenny would urge him to stay home. "If they fire you, you can always get another job," she would coax. Kevin began to lose job after job and to move from place to place when the overdue rent mounted up.

When Jenny discovered she was pregnant, Kevin married her. He felt they should begin living a calmer life, one that would be healthier for raising children, but Jenny was too restless. Within the space of four years, they had three children, but motherhood never slowed down the party-loving Jenny. Her erratic behavior—leaving Kevin and the kids for long periods of time to party with friends—interfered with Kevin's attempts to create stability for his family. When her third child was only a few months old, Jenny left Kevin and the children once again. This time Kevin didn't want her back.

Barely into his 20s, with three tiny, dependent children to care for, Kevin realized he had to become a responsible adult. He would need to find a decent full-time job—and be sure to keep it. After some searching, he landed a job at a plant that produced Styrofoam cups. He'd had some experience in previous jobs as a machinist, so the plant hired him for this skilled position.

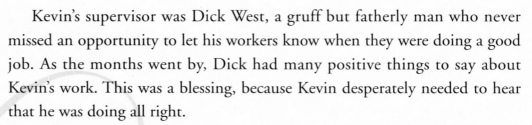

Kevin's supervisor was Dick West, a gruff but fatherly man who never missed an opportunity to let his workers know when they were doing a good job. As the months went by, Dick had many positive things to say about Kevin's work. This was a blessing, because Kevin desperately needed to hear that he was doing all right.

Kevin wasn't used to holding a job for more than a few months at a time. The daily grind made him impatient. He had to rise early and take his children to the babysitter before heading to the plant to put in a long day. Then he came home to make supper, do laundry, bathe the children, and read bedtime stories. He fantasized a thousand times about quitting his job and sleeping in as late as the kids would let him.

But he couldn't disappoint Dick. Dick said Kevin was a fast learner, a careful and precise worker, the best machinist they'd had in a long time. And Dick cared about how things were going with Kevin. He asked Kevin about his three children. He chuckled at stories about mischievous things they'd done and comical things they'd said. He commiserated with Kevin about the everyday trials of broken water heaters and cars that refused to start. "It won't always be like this," Dick insisted. "Things will get better. I was a single dad myself, in a situation like yours. But I survived—and you will, too."

Two days before Christmas, Kevin was at work, busily honing a tool, when Dick walked up to him. "I have a delivery to make outside the plant. Why don't you come along?" Kevin was puzzled; he'd never been asked to do this kind of work before. But if Dick needed help, he was happy to pitch in. Soon they were leaving the plant in a pickup truck. Kevin couldn't see what the truck held; its cargo was covered by a tarpaulin.

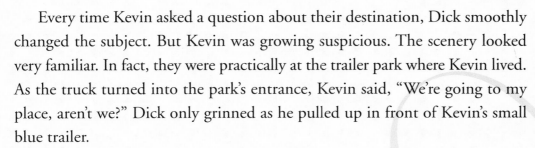

Every time Kevin asked a question about their destination, Dick smoothly changed the subject. But Kevin was growing suspicious. The scenery looked very familiar. In fact, they were practically at the trailer park where Kevin lived. As the truck turned into the park's entrance, Kevin said, "We're going to my place, aren't we?" Dick only grinned as he pulled up in front of Kevin's small blue trailer.

When the tarpaulin came off of the truck, Kevin stared in amazement. The truck bed was loaded with brightly wrapped Christmas presents, tricycles for the kids, and enough fixings to make several holiday dinners. There was even a real Christmas tree.

Every year at Christmas, the factory chose several families of employees who could use an extra boost. Dick had submitted Kevin's name and then discreetly collected all the information Santa's elves needed, such as the children's ages, interests, and clothing sizes.

The Christmas truck was a turning point in Kevin's life because it brought more than gifts. It proved to him that someone recognized his potential and his hard work—that someone believed in him. Today, Kevin is the chief machinist in his division, and he owns his own home. His life has become more secure in other ways, too. Soon after that Christmas, he began attending church and received a calling to study for the ministry. Kevin has just been ordained as the pastor of his own church, where his mission is to offer others the belief that turned his own life around.

BY ANN RUSSELL

The Gift That Keeps on Giving Me Trouble

IN ONE CHURCH that I pastored several years ago, we had a young lad in the Sunday school named Jimmy Foxx. His father had died, and Jimmy's mother did her best to raise him. She did not have an easy job because Jimmy was mentally challenged. Although 15 at the time, his mental capacity was that of an eight-year-old.

When the Foxxes came to our church, everyone immediately took them into their hearts. At the time, people did not understand Jimmy's condition. Yet the people accepted Jimmy and his mother into the congregation, and they blended in quite well.

Once, we had an evangelist in our church for a week of special services. Jimmy took an immediate liking to him and never missed a service. Everything went fine until one Thursday evening. The evangelist preached: "Take us the foxes, the little foxes, that spoil the vines: for our vines have tender grapes" (Song of Songs 2:15 KJV). In developing his sermon, the evangelist emphasized that the "little foxes" in our life do much damage.

Jimmy always sat in the front pew, and from my seat I could watch him. I began to notice something was terribly wrong. Suddenly, in a burst of tears, he got up and ran out of the church building.

Jimmy lived just three blocks from the church, and I followed him home. I went into Jimmy's room and found him lying on his bed sobbing, as though his heart would break.

When I calmed him down some, I asked him what was wrong.

"That preacher hates me," Jimmy said.

"No, he doesn't hate you, Jimmy," I assured him.

"Yes, he does."

At this point, I did not know what was going through his mind. "What makes you think that, Jimmy?" I asked.

"He said foxes were bad. I heard him, and I'm a Foxx and he said I was bad. That preacher hates me."

It finally dawned on me what had happened. It took several hours to calm him down and explain what the evangelist meant. I do not know if he ever understood, but Jimmy trusted me and came back the next night.

For some reason, Jimmy liked me. I guess it was because he had no father and I tried to spend time with him.

As Christmas drew near that year, Jimmy became more excited than usual.

"Reverend," he squealed, "my mother said I can get you a Christmas present." His beaming face beguiled the impending trouble. Not knowing this, I smiled and said, "That's great Jimmy. I can't wait." With that, Jimmy laughed.

There is a reason God does not allow us to see into the future, and this Christmas gift of Jimmy's proved the point. When Jimmy came to the church Christmas party, he beamed with excitement. He came to me and said, "I got it, Reverend! I got it!" "What did you get, Jimmy?" I asked.

Then he laughed and said, "You'll see, Reverend! You'll see!"

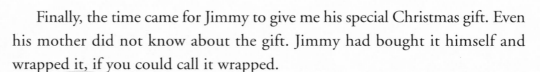

Finally, the time came for Jimmy to give me his special Christmas gift. Even his mother did not know about the gift. Jimmy had bought it himself and wrapped it, if you could call it wrapped.

I must say that I have received many gifts in my time, but this gift from Jimmy was the most unique gift I had ever received. Much thought had gone into this gift. Jimmy knew I liked ties and wore them all the time. As I unwrapped Jimmy's gift, I got a glimpse of the tie.

It was unlike any tie I had ever seen. I knew Jimmy was watching my face to see if I liked his gift. As I proudly held the tie up to an audience of suppressed giggles, Jimmy exploded in a mixture of laughter and clapping.

"Do you like it, Reverend?" he asked. Then he added: "I can't wait for you to wear my tie to church this Sunday."

What does a minister do with a fluorescent orange tie with a picture of a hula dancer? On what occasion does a preacher wear such a tie? More important, do I worry about matching socks? I found myself in a dilemma.

I had a choice. I could hurt Jimmy's feelings and not wear the tie on Sunday. Or, I could swallow my pride and wear it to his everlasting delight. What do I drink to wash down my pride?

This incident helped me understand what the Apostle Paul meant when he wrote, "I have showed you all things, how that so labouring ye ought to support the weak, and to remember the words of the Lord Jesus, how he said, It is more blessed to give than to receive" (Acts 20:35 KJV).

Some gifts are important because of who gives them. And yes, I wore the tie on Sunday.

By Rev. James L. Snyder

The Cross on the Window

❦ ❦ ❦

I STOOD BEHIND the counter observing the stone-faced men, women, and children enter the silent waiting area and take their places on the long, narrow wooden bench.

Why am I in this awful place during Christmas week? I wondered.

Back in my suburban home, packages waited to be wrapped, pies needed to be baked, and I had a turkey to prepare. But I was dropping giveaway groceries into brown paper bags for society's destitute.

I didn't want to be in this musty-smelling food pantry in the inner city with these pale, sad-eyed people. And they knew it. Embarrassed, they would look down and search the old Formica countertop as I silently read their requisitions.

A fellow church member scheduled to serve in the food pantry had been called out of town. In a weak moment, I had agreed to take his place. Now there I was, face to face with pregnant teens without wedding bands and listless children wearing hopelessness in their dull eyes.

I was angry. I wanted to go home. The poor before me sensed my displeasure, and I did nothing to soften their discomfort.

"Pardon me, ma'am," a raspy voice said.

I turned to face a shivering young man in a thin jacket, his hands dug deeply into the pockets of his worn jeans.

"Yes?" I asked, looking past him.

He sniffled. "My kids," he said softly. "I ain't got nothin' to feed'm."

My first reaction was to tell him to take his place on the bench, but as I surveyed the weary crowd waiting in melancholy silence, I was aware they were content to sit absorbing the warm air flowing from the register. They had no place to go, I told myself. No jobs, certainly no Christmas shopping to do, and no cookies to bake.

I swallowed hard at the jittery man before me. At least he was clean, I thought, and he didn't smell of alcohol or tobacco like so many of the clients.

"Do you have a requisition?" I asked.

"No, ma'am." He shook his head slowly. "I came in because I saw the cross on the window."

I sighed and shifted my weight from one foot to the other. "You have to have a…" I stopped in the middle of my sentence and looked at the slumped-shouldered man across the counter, then at the row of society's shunned huddling on the bench. There was no place for this man to sit.

My eyes met the eyes of a frail little girl. She quickly looked away, burying her face in her mother's shoulder.

I suddenly felt their despair.

In my selfishness, I had forgotten that these were people in need. It was clear they didn't want to ask for handouts, but they had no choice. Their kids were hungry.

Sometimes the recipients had a few coins and would stop by the heaping tables of used clothing and odds and ends in the back of the store to purchase materials given by "church people."

"We don't run this shop for profit. We charge a mite to protect people's dignity," the pastor in charge had said. "Serve them with kindness and respect," he reminded the volunteers.

"How many children?" I asked the young man, suddenly feeling ashamed.

"Five."

"Adults?" I asked.

He shook his head. "Jus' me, and I don't need nothin'."

"Of course you do!" I said. "Your wife?"

He shook his head sadly. "She died a while back." His voice broke. "There's just the kids and me."

"What about Christmas?" I asked, swallowing my tears. "Santa?"

He smiled sadly. "I told'm Santa wouldn't be around this year. They understand."

How could a child understand no visit from Santa? I wondered, gathering the food. As I set the rattling bags on the counter, the metal cross hanging from my neck clanged against the Formica. The words of the pastor echoed in my brain: "Treat them with kindness and respect."

He nodded to my cross. "I didn't know where else to go 'cept the church." His eyes welled up.

I smiled and touched his trembling hand. "You did right."

"Thanks," he said, looking deep into my eyes. "I'm tryin' to find work."

"I know," I said, scratching a note to the volunteers at the back of the store. "They'll help you find something for the kids for Christmas."

"I can't take nothin' like that," he said softly.

"It's for the kids," I insisted.

His quiet eyes brightened. "Thanks," he said, gathering up his bags as he headed to the back of the store. "Merry Christmas!" he called, straightening his shoulders.

"Merry Christmas!" I called cheerfully.

I smiled, then faced the room of forlorn faces. "Next!" I called happily.

Though the people I helped that day walked away with bags of much-needed food, they gave me something much more valuable: a lesson in dignity and respect.

BY CAROL KEHLMEIER

HARK! THE HERALD ANGELS SING

Hark! The herald angels sing,
"Glory to the new-born King,
Peace on earth and mercy mild
God and sinners reconciled."
Joyful all ye nations rise,
Join the triumph of the skies.
With th' angelic host proclaim.
"Christ is born in Bethlehem."

CHARLES WESLEY

The Batman Bike

❦   ❦   ❦

I WAS A SINGLE MOTHER, and my son was three years old. Struggling to attend college full-time and also work to support us, there was never any money left over. Christmas was fast approaching, and with my meager resources, it was looking bleak.

More than anything, my son wanted a Batman bike. With its tiny frame and little training wheels, he longed to ride it like the "big" boys. And I longed to give it to him. It really wasn't too much to ask for. I watched as my friends bought piles of presents for their children, knowing that a tiny bike wouldn't even faze their checking accounts, let alone deplete them as it would mine.

Searching frantically for ways to earn extra money, I became more and more hopeless that I would ever be able to provide the one thing my small son wanted. He talked constantly about the Batman bike that Santa would bring him, and my heart ached each time it came up.

Cramming for finals, caring for my child alone, and working in between had me frazzled and despondent. One late December night, I took a break from my studying and went to check on my sleeping toddler. Looking at his rosy lips, angel-soft hair, and the long eyelashes that kissed his cheeks, I knew I had to find a way. I knelt down gently beside my tiny son and began to pray.

I told God that I knew the bike was a material thing and that in the grand scheme of things, it was unimportant. I also told him that as Nicholas's mother, my job was to provide for my little guy. I told him that I knew Christmas was about the birth of his son, and that I would always teach that to my child. I said that if there was a way for me to grant this wish for Nicholas, that I would work hard, sacrifice anything I could. But I needed help. If it were his will, he would have to help me.

I had a short break from school for the holidays, and finals were behind me, so I began to look for extra work. The tricky part was that it had to be something I could do at home—or at least do with Nicholas with me. Jobs like that were not easy to find. Luckily, I found work at Nicholas's day care, which also enabled me to be with him during the day, and I tended to other day-care children whenever I could. I finally had enough money to put the bike on layaway, but what would happen if I couldn't pay it off?

I was afraid to hope for this bike. I felt so ineffective and a failure at providing for my son. The prayers continued fervently, and slowly I came up with more ways of earning Christmas money. I began to do ironing for a neighbor, who then sent her friends to me as well. The thing was, I hate to iron. I don't just dislike it—I hate it. I'd rather have my wisdom teeth pulled. But iron I did. Late every night, I would iron and starch and iron and starch until my apartment was filled with other people's neatly pressed clothes. Even though I hated it, I knew it was a gift of love for my son. And the money built up, bit by bit.

I began to look forward to Christmas even more than my son did. As I worked frantically to scrimp together enough money for the teeny bike, my understanding of parental sacrifice deepened. It was a lesson on many levels.

I made the payments on his bike until it was nearly paid off. The day I knew I had enough, I cried. All that ironing that I detested was worth it a million times over. I was blessed tenfold. I had enough for a few other small presents and stocking-stuffers. My father bought us a wonderful Christmas tree, and it was perfect. He knew what I had just learned. My heart swelled with sweet pride that only a parent can know. Sacrifice for one's child is the purest and most rewarding expression of love.

BY SUSAN FAHNCKE

SILENT NIGHT

Silent night, holy night!
All is calm, all is bright.
Round yon Virgin, Mother and Child.
Holy infant so tender and mild,
Sleep in heavenly peace,
Sleep in heavenly peace.

Silent night, holy night!
Shepherds quake at the sight.
Glories stream from heaven afar
Heavenly hosts sing Alleluia,

Christ the Savior is born!
Christ the Savior is born.

Silent night, holy night!
Son of God love's pure light.
Radiant beams from Thy holy face
With dawn of redeeming grace,
Jesus Lord, at Thy birth.
Jesus Lord, at Thy birth.

JOSEPH MOHR (1792–1848)

Ripples of Love

ON CHRISTMAS EVE, a message was left on Hope's answering machine: "My name is Merlene. I have a package here that I think belongs to you. Please give me a call." She then left her number.

That evening, Hope called Merlene. Merlene explained that a package had come to her mailbox by mistake. She said she could barely read the name on the label, but with the help of a magnifying glass, and by looking in the phone book, she believed she had found the rightful owner.

Hope and her husband, Bertram, arranged to pick up the errant package that evening. They knew their daughter, Alison, would be relieved to hear they had finally received it.

They located Merlene in a vintage apartment complex. Hope waited in the car while Bertram went to get the package. Merlene, a pleasant, comely woman in her 40s, introduced herself and her ten-year-old son, Jonathan.

"We apologize for opening the box. My son and the boy I babysit opened it, thinking it was ours." Merlene had resealed the package.

Bertram glanced around the tidy room. He noted the well-worn rug and sofa and the dimly lit lamp in the corner, but he saw no sign of Christmas.

"We won't be having a Christmas this year," Merlene told him, as if reading Bertram's mind. "My son and I have been in a financial crunch lately, so we're forgoing a tree and gifts this year."

Alison always sent beautiful gifts, purchased from an upscale department store, so Hope and Bertram could exchange them, if needed. Bertram knew that Merlene could have kept the package and returned the merchandise for money.

With many thanks, Bertram put the package under his arm and went out to the car. Merlene followed him out to meet Hope and say goodbye. Before pulling away, Bertram got out of the car, pressed something into Merlene's hand, and closed her fingers over it. He quickly got back in the car, put up the window while waving goodbye, and drove away.

Later that evening, Hope phoned her sister, Nancy, in California and told her about the incident. As Nancy listened, she felt moved to do something for Merlene and her son.

Nancy wrote to Merlene using the sketchy information that Hope had given her. Hope had only Merlene's first name and part of an address. With a prayer in her heart, Nancy wrote:

"Dear Merlene,

"We haven't met, but you've met my sister and her husband when a package destined for them was mistakenly delivered to your house. Hearing Hope's story of your honesty touched our hearts! So, in the spirit of giving, we'd like to spread Christmas around to more than our family. Please take this token of money and use it as you see fit. God has blessed us, and we want to share his goodness with you and your son. God bless you.

"Nancy and Joe Denson."

Merlene did receive Nancy's letter and promptly responded:

"Dear Nancy and Joe,

"How wonderful are the Lord's blessings, and how mysterious are his ways. I am a single parent of a ten-year-old son. I've been trying the best I can to tell him that honesty is always the best policy, no matter what. Not because of any earthly rewards, but because it's the honorable way.

"It's amazing how far the story of this little act of honesty has gone and the blessings it has brought. My son and I live in a neighborhood where, unfortunately, acts of kindness aren't usually appreciated. Not even with a simple 'thank you.' My son says, 'Why do things for other people, then?' I simply think it's the right thing to do.

"Your letter and gift are helping my son realize that while we sure didn't expect a reward for our actions, sometimes the Lord uses others to help provide blessings. Your dollars went immediately to the grocery store. Thank you for your generosity and the memories we now have because of it. I guess the Lord really is listening and knows our needs.

"May your New Year be filled with a new closeness to our Lord and Savior. God Bless.

"Sincerely, Merlene and Jonathan."

The story does not end here. Since that Christmas exchange, other family members have written notes and given gifts of encouragement to Merlene and Jonathan. Alison's fiancé was touched by this episode and sent Merlene a gift, as did Nancy's children, brother, and other members of the family.

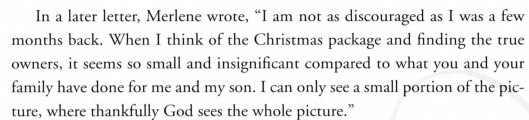

In a later letter, Merlene wrote, "I am not as discouraged as I was a few months back. When I think of the Christmas package and finding the true owners, it seems so small and insignificant compared to what you and your family have done for me and my son. I can only see a small portion of the picture, where thankfully God sees the whole picture."

Our family determined that the next Christmas would be different. Gift-giving would include Merlene and Jonathan, as well as other people like them. Just like throwing a pebble into a pond, the ripples keep spreading ever outward.

BY JANET RODDA

And the angel said to [the shepherds], "Be not afraid; for behold, I bring you good news of a great joy which will come to all the people; for to you is born this day in the city of David a Savior, who is Christ the Lord. And this will be a sign for you: you will find a babe wrapped in swaddling cloths and lying in a manger." And suddenly there was with the angel a multitude of the heavenly host praising God and saying, "Glory to God in the highest, and on earth peace among men with whom he is pleased!"...And they went with haste, and found Mary and Joseph, and the babe lying in a manger.

LUKE 2:10–14, 16

Unlimited Hugs

Young Kevin paced the floor of his room, and no matter how many times he checked, his piggy bank was still empty. He had set his heart on getting Mom a Christmas gift, the best gift ever. How could he do that now that he had foolishly spent all of his money?

There must be a way. And, after much thought, he had it. He'd create a coupon for Mom, the best coupon ever. He put all of his concentration into that coupon, every bit of creativity in him. And the coupon, when he finished it, was wonderful—brightly colored, neat, and clear, his absolute best work ever.

"Kev, this is wonderful!" Mom said as she opened the gift on Christmas morning. Kevin grinned happily. "The best gift I've ever gotten—and so well done! What a great job you did on it!"

Mom then claimed her first hug, for the coupon promised unlimited hugs, as many as she wanted, always. Mom taped the coupon to her kitchen cabinet and used it often, getting Kevin's very best, super-tight, mighty bear hugs.

One thing about Mom: She always enjoyed the gifts Kevin gave her, whether homemade or store-bought. He enjoyed watching the joy light up her face, the tenderness brighten her eyes. She didn't fake it, either, pretending to be crazy about it . . . then burying it under socks in a drawer. Mom wore every silly necklace Kevin made her out of macaroni, and she used every lumpy vase he shaped from soggy clay.

Years slipped by, and Kevin became a teen, often cranky, snapping at Mom instead of joking with her, complaining more often than he smiled.

At Christmas, Kevin sometimes forgot to give Mom a gift at all. Or he bought her a package of socks. Once he gave her a broom. But that didn't bother her. Because whenever Kevin got especially cranky and bad-tempered, Mom had her secret weapon. A bit worn, limp from great use, and tattered around the edges, the unlimited-hugs coupon still hung from Mom's kitchen cabinet door. When Kevin griped and fussed, Mom just turned around, reached for the coupon, and held it out to Kevin.

"Ah, Mom," Kevin would moan, "not that old thing."

Mom never argued or fussed back at him. She held out the coupon and waited. Then Kevin, face turning pink with embarrassment, would bend down from his new height and hug his mom. No matter how irritable he'd been. No matter how annoyed or unhappy he had acted. Kevin always honored that battered old coupon.

And anyone who ever asked Kevin's mom about the best Christmas gift she'd ever received got the same response. She never hesitated, never paused to ponder, never had a moment's doubt.

She'd hold out that brightly colored coupon, smiling and maybe a bit teary-eyed. "Best gift I ever got," she claimed, and everyone knew she meant it.

By Kara Quinn

Christmas Angels

LOVE CAME DOWN at Christmas,
Love all lovely, Love Divine;
Love was born at Christmas;
Star and angels gave the sign.

CHRISTINA ROSSETTI (1830–1894)

You Are Beautiful

❦   ❦   ❦

NOT MANY PEOPLE talk to my son. It isn't that they don't want to. Everyone who sees him wishes they could. There is something so rare and beautiful about him. I know, I'm his mother and I'm supposed to think that, but strangers often come up to me and just announce how beautiful he is. Instead of saying "thank you" like any well-mannered mother would, I always look at his beautiful chubby face, with its rosy cheeks, brilliant blue eyes, full red lips, and, in awe myself, I simply say, "I know." Something within him bubbles over with life, amazing even me.

My son is two years old. And he is deaf.

I used to become embarrassed when strangers would stare at our conversations. My hands flying, my face animated to express my "tone of voice," and my toddler's chubby hands fluttering with his baby signs, his face even more animated than mine. I know it is something to see.

But embarrassment soon became pride when I realized that people were only staring because they thought our language was beautiful. Indeed it is. Many times I have watched with joy, my heart bursting with pride and sheer love, when I've seen my baby speak with his hands. He can say more with his hands and his face than most children his age can say with their voices. To me, nothing is more endearing than a child's small hands signing "I love you" or "Mama, hold me."

People will walk up to us, sometimes embarrassed and nervous, sometimes shy, but always curious about this beautiful language we use. Time and time again, I am asked where they can learn to sign. What I used to mistake for rudeness was simply admiration and the wishing of strangers that they could speak like us.

However much they want to, most of the people in my little son's life cannot speak to him. As a result, he goes through life in a silent confusion, with only a very small percentage of the people he comes in contact with able to communicate with him.

And when we do meet someone who "speaks" his language, it is a unique and wonderful gift.

Last December, just before Christmas, our family went to a nearby café. We were enjoying each other's company, laughing and talking together. The place was filling up fast with the holiday crowd, and, as usual, I noticed many people watching us sign.

Near the front door were two missionaries, young men dressed in suits. One of them was staring intently at my conversation with my son. My son and I were laughing together as I signed "piggy," and he was complying by slurping down his hot cocoa. Making a whipped cream beard on his little chin, he signed "Santa" and had our whole family laughing.

The young missionary waited for my toddler to turn his head, and when he did, the young man waved

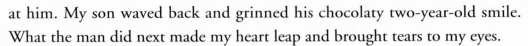

at him. My son waved back and grinned his chocolaty two-year-old smile. What the man did next made my heart leap and brought tears to my eyes.

I watched with amazement as his hands formed the signs for "you are beautiful." I choked back a sob and watched as he did it again. My beautiful child turned and looked at me, his blue eyes huge, as if to say, "Mom, did you see that?!" I pointed to the young missionary and then showed my son the sign for "friend." The young man then signed to my son, "How are you?" Grinning with delight, my son did a few baby signs back and, being two, that was the extent of his attention span.

Smiling shyly, the young man told me that his sister was fluent in American Sign Language, and over the years he had picked up on it. We made polite conversation, and all too soon it was time to leave. We fondly wished each other a Merry Christmas, sharing a moment that most people would not understand.

Although I'll never see that young man again, for a brief moment he gave me a gift I will never forget. His conversation with my son was like a ray of sunshine in the midst of a snowy night. Remembering his hands telling my child he is beautiful in his own language still brings the tears. There aren't many moments like that for him, and I will savor the memory always.

BY SUSAN FAHNCKE

My Very Best Friends

❧ ❧ ❧

WALLY TOWNSEND, NOW 74, stoop-shouldered and slow afoot, was hardly conscious of the snow falling around him as he led Shadow, his nearly blind dog, on her morning neighborhood walk.

Wally couldn't stop thinking about last Christmas. That was the day they had a big family celebration. That was the day Martha gave him an expensive black suit and he gave her a fur coat. That was the day they would spend their last Christmas together, for two weeks later, Martha, his wife of 42 years, was dead, the victim of congestive heart failure.

Now it was Christmas a year later, and the memories of Martha still lingered in Wally's mind as if it were yesterday. Even now, while walking his dog, Wally saw a vision of Martha in the reflection of the snow, and for a moment his heart stood still. He wished she were still alive so he could take her in his arms again and tell her how much he loved her.

He thought about his daughter, Jenny, his only child, and how disappointed she was when he called her the previous night. "I won't be able to make it up to your house tomorrow," Wally told her. "The roads are iced over up your way."

"I know, Dad," Jenny said. "We're having a blizzard up here, but I hate for you to spend Christmas alone. Can you have dinner with Marge and Harvey or some of your church friends?"

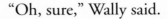

"Oh, sure," Wally said.

"Promise?" Jenny asked.

"Don't worry about me. I'll be fine," Wally said.

"Well, since you're not coming up, I may as well tell you what I got with the check you sent us," said Jenny. "I got Bob a pair of boots. I got April a heart-shaped diamond necklace she's been wanting, and I got some cookware for the whole family. We're going to have a great Christmas thanks to you, but we'll miss you not being here with us."

Wally hated to miss spending Christmas with Jenny and April, his 14-year-old granddaughter, and even Bob, his talkative son-in-law. But the roads were too dangerous to travel, Wally reasoned. Of course, there were plenty of places he could go today, Wally thought, but Christmas was for families and he didn't want to intrude. Maybe it was just as well that he stayed home, Wally concluded, because he didn't have much Christmas spirit anyway.

The ground was almost covered with snow now. Martha would have loved having a white Christmas, Wally thought, as he led Shadow up the driveway of his modest brick home. Wally pulled off his stocking cap and waved at first one and then another of his neighbors as they drove by. Before he retired, Wally served 32 years as a teacher in the local school system, and nearly everybody in the community knew him.

Wally took off Shadow's leash and doggie coat out in the garage, then went into the house to dress. Martha believed in dressing up for Christmas dinner. That was one way to honor the Lord, she always said.

Wally put on a white shirt and bright red tie and then slipped on the black suit Martha gave him. He combed his full crop of unruly gray hair until there was not a strand out of place. He paused and examined himself in the mirror. He wondered if Martha would think he looked handsome.

At precisely 12:30, Wally laid out his best silverware and fancy tablecloth, which Martha had used only on special occasions. He set two plates on the table along with the small amount of food he prepared. He cut a strip of cardboard from the back of an old shoe box. Using a colored drawing pencil, he printed the word "Jesus" on the strip of cardboard and propped it up in front of the plate at the head of the table.

Next, he turned on the chandelier lights that hung overhead. He looked at Shadow, his 13-year-old cocker spaniel, sitting on the floor beside him.

He closed his eyes, and for a moment he visualized Jesus sitting before him. Jesus wore a white robe. His eyes glistened and he seemed to have a warm, compassionate smile on his face.

"Happy birthday, Jesus," Wally began. "I'm honored to have you with us on this special day. I know you're not here in person, but you're here in spirit. I know because I can feel your presence."

He paused, trying to think of what to say, because this was all spontaneous. "Tell Martha how much Shadow and I miss her. Shadow still roams through the house every day looking for her, and so do I," he said as his voice shook.

"I want to thank you for allowing me to have 42 years with Martha," Wally said. "She was an angel on earth, and now she's an angel with you."

He paused to wipe away a tear. "You can tell Martha that I still sit in the center section, third row at church and I still reserve her a seat. Last Sunday they sang that old hymn, 'Victory in Jesus,' and I could still hear her voice ring out above all the others."

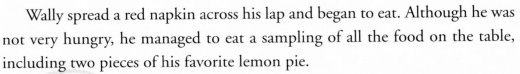

Wally spread a red napkin across his lap and began to eat. Although he was not very hungry, he managed to eat a sampling of all the food on the table, including two pieces of his favorite lemon pie.

Later that evening, after he had cleared the table and put the dishes in the dishwasher, he settled down by the fireplace in his favorite rocking chair. He had just got comfortable when the phone rang.

"Merry Christmas," said Bob. "Thank you for the boots, man. They'll come in handy with all the snow and ice we're having."

"Merry Christmas, Grandpa. Merry Christmas, Shadow," said April. "Thank you for the necklace. I just love it."

"Dad, April and Bob are on the extension," said Jenny. "We've got a house full of company and I can hardly hear you."

"Christmas isn't the same without you, Dad," said Jenny.

"Yeah, my Christmas was a little different this year, too," said Wally.

"Did you have dinner with your friends?" Jenny asked.

"Oh, yes," said Wally. "Yes, as a matter of fact I did."

"Oh, good. I was so worried about you," said Jenny. "Well, listen, Dad, Bob's folks are here so I'd better go. I'll call you later tonight."

"I love you, Grandpa, and thanks to you I had a super Christmas," said April.

"I love you, too," Wally said as he heard the click of the phone hanging up. *I had a super Christmas, too,* Wally thought, smiling to himself. *I had dinner with my very best friends.*

BY BRUCE ADKINS

Special Delivery

❦ ❦ ❦

As Bob and I stepped into a hospital for the chronically ill, our daughters—Suzanne, six, and Jennifer, three—vied to push the button that would start us upward. The elevator groaned into motion. I suddenly had second thoughts about bringing the girls here. Would they be frightened? Was this expecting too much of them? Maybe, as in past years, we should have simply taken a name from the church's giving tree, bought and wrapped the requested gift, and placed it under the tree for someone else to deliver.

But when we had approached the tag-laden giving tree two weeks before, a thought had come to me: These aren't just tags! They represent real people with real needs. Who would we be giving a gift to? A prisoner? A nursing home resident? A needy child in the inner city?

With each passing year, I was becoming more uncomfortable with the way we celebrated Christ's birth. I longed to teach the girls how to give without expecting anything in return. Maybe by delivering the gifts ourselves, we would all learn something about Christmas.

The elevator doors creaked open. The odor of urine and disinfectant was hanging in the air. We stepped onto a shiny black-and-white checkered floor and followed the dizzying pattern down a long hallway.

Suzanne and Jennifer peered into the rooms. Each contained a panorama of pain where tubes, bottles, and machines extended lives and gave hope.

We stopped at the doorway of room 312. A petite woman in a wheelchair greeted us. "Hi! I'm Terry Cournoyer." She smiled as we introduced ourselves. She raised a limp hand as she accepted the gift we brought her, the one she'd asked for on the giving-tree tag.

"Thanks a lot," she said. "I'd like to wait and open it on Christmas Eve if you don't mind."

Several dolls propped on Terry's red, green, and white crocheted bedspread caught the girls' attention. A potpourri of ceramic cats, stuffed animals, and trinkets sat on a tall bookcase. The bottom shelf held a variety of games and books, including several versions of the Bible. Photographs decorated the dingy white walls.

Terry told us that from a family of nine children, she was the only one still living. She had no relatives to visit her. As she talked, I reached into my purse and offered her some candy.

"Oh, I'd love to," she said, "but I haven't eaten anything in 16 years."

Suzanne and Jennifer turned and stared. "Aren't you hungry?" Suzanne wanted to know.

"No, not at all," Terry answered. "The nurse feeds me through a tube that goes right into my stomach. I have multiple sclerosis, and I can't swallow. But when I get to heaven I'm going to enjoy a huge, juicy hamburger."

As we prepared to leave, I found myself saying, "I see you have a Scrabble game. Maybe I could come back and play with you sometime."

"I'd like that," Terry answered.

On the way home, Bob asked me, "How come you didn't set a definite date to play Scrabble with Terry?"

"Well, I know how disappointed patients get when someone promises to come and then doesn't," I said. But I laid awake that night thinking about Terry. I knew I had to put legs on my faith. After all, when God delivered his gift, that wasn't the end of it. The Bible says, "And the Word became flesh and dwelt among us, and we beheld His glory…" (John 1:14a, NKJV).

A few days later, I found myself back in Terry's room. I set up a folding chair next to her wheelchair, and we chatted as we set up the game. But the conversation flowed so well, we never did get around to playing Scrabble.

Terry told me that her best friend, Gail, a young paralyzed woman, lived three rooms away. Gail's mother often brought tapes of our church services to her daughter and to Terry. "I love the Lord," Terry said, "and I would like to attend your church."

After thinking a moment, I realized I could help make it happen. "Let's try," I said enthusiastically. "We can use the Share-A-Ride service. They are equipped to transport your wheelchair."

We started bringing Terry to church once a month. Later, we added trips to the mall. Then Bob and the girls joined me in making regular visits to see Terry.

Soon, Terry was like a part of our family. The girls grew fond of her, and she, in turn, thrived on their abundant hugs and kisses. When Bob discovered that Terry was an avid sports fan, he planned a special outing to a Celtics game.

When Suzanne turned seven, she wanted Terry to attend her birthday party. Bob picked her up and brought her to our house. Later, as I emptied Terry's

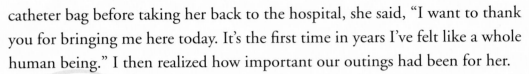

catheter bag before taking her back to the hospital, she said, "I want to thank you for bringing me here today. It's the first time in years I've felt like a whole human being." I then realized how important our outings had been for her.

One day while I was at the hospital, Terry started talking to me about her health situation. "For someone who's had MS for as long as I have, doctors are amazed at how high-functioning I am," she said. "I've seen others come and go, but I'm still going strong. While I'm able, I'd like to prepare for the time when I'll go home to be with the Lord. Diane, will you be the one to make the arrangements for me?"

"Of course," I said, swallowing a lump in my throat. I didn't want to think of losing Terry. She had taught me how to give. Though she was legally blind and unable to walk, swallow, or do anything for herself, Terry would ride around in her wheelchair recruiting patients for the Friday night Bible study. When she listened to her Bible tapes, she turned the volume up so that others could hear the message, too.

Terry had wanted to be a medical missionary. I told her that she was. Every day she would pray, "Please use me today," and God did.

As our second Christmas with Terry drew near, we expected that she would join us for Christmas Day, since we knew how much she looked forward to her times outside the hospital. Instead, she declined our invitation.

"I can't leave Gail alone on Christmas," she explained.

So after our Christmas Eve church service, we went to visit Terry. The girls had painted sweatshirts for her, writing in sparkling glitter on the sleeves, "I love you, Terry." The sparkle in their eyes matched the shimmer on the shirts as they gave their gifts to Terry.

But Terry had given us much more than we could ever give her. I knew that our family would never again be limited to the swap-a-gift-of-equal-value routine. Just a year ago, we had gone to her room delivering a simple present, and there we had found God's presence. For through this woman who prays every day to be used, we encountered the divine, and we learned the true meaning of Christmas.

BY DIANE ZICKELL, AS TOLD TO PRISCILLA LARSON

IT CAME UPON A MIDNIGHT CLEAR

It came upon a midnight clear,
That glorious song of old,
From angels bending near the earth
To touch their harps of gold:
"Peace on the earth, good will to men,
From heav'n's all-gracious King."
The world in solemn stillness lay
To hear the angels sing.

WORDS BY EDMUND SEARS (1810–1876)
MUSIC BY RICHARD S. WILLIS (1819–1900)

Timmy

❧   ❧   ❧

WHEN MY BABY BROTHER, Timmy, was born with Down's syndrome, we thought he would be trouble. He surprised us and grew into a wonderful, beautiful young man who filled our lives with happiness.

When I got married and left home, I moved only about 30 miles away. Visiting meant playing games, going on picnics, and skipping rocks in the river with Timmy. We visited often.

Those visits were wonderful because Timmy was a very loving person and had many interests, most of which he excelled at. Even though he couldn't read or write, he could play basketball, and he could beat us all at target shooting.

Timmy was imaginative and could find fun in anything. He often chose to play with just blocks of wood. He even had calluses on his fingers from handling wood so much. He pretended that the wood blocks were cars or trucks, and he would build houses with them. He hardly ever asked for toys, and he took good care of the things that were given to him, including his hats. Timmy loved hats; he had many caps and little hats that had been given to him as presents.

Never did we dream that Timmy would get leukemia. For him to be so deathly ill was beyond anything we could have ever imagined. He was so sweet, and he had never done anything wrong. *Why?* We all kept asking the same big question. *Why?*

He's too young, we thought. *He's only 23 years old.* Considering he had the mind of a three- or four-year-old, can you imagine how frightened he was with all the probing doctors, big machines, and harsh treatments he had to endure?

We had taken him to a small hospital near the town where we lived. The doctors sent him straight to a bigger hospital—at the University of Virginia. My oldest sister rode with him in an ambulance. It was a long, horrid ride.

Timmy endured his stay in the hospital. Unfortunately, our mother was sick at the time, so we took turns staying in the hospital with Timmy. One of us was at his side at all times. We bathed him, fed him, and did everything else we could for him. Timmy was homesick, but we called home every night so he could talk to Mom. He tried so hard to be brave, but often he ended up in tears.

The nurses and doctors were good to him, and he made many friends during the time he was there. We have an album full of pictures of him—and photos of nurses and doctors, too.

On days when Timmy felt well, he loved to goof around, showing off for his friends. He would put on a pair of tennis shoes and do the moonwalk down the hospital hall, pretending to be Michael Jackson. Everyone always clapped and made a fuss over him. Timmy loved the attention.

The nurses were always bringing him goodies. Sometimes he didn't have an appetite and would go for long periods without eating. Everyone tried bringing different meals to see if Timmy would eat.

A month before Christmas, we started asking Timmy what he wanted Santa to bring him. Maybe a new cap or a pair of tennis shoes? He never answered.

Then, on Christmas Eve, he surprised everyone by saying, "I'd like a red fire truck." That night it snowed something fierce. We were not prepared for this. All the stores surrounding the hospital were closed. We went to the gift shop downstairs, but no red fire trucks. On Christmas Day, we let Timmy open his presents, which included new tennis shoes, a new cap, and a few small toys. He never once mentioned missing the red fire truck.

About an hour later, someone knocked on the door. When I answered it, a handsome, tall doctor asked, "Is this Timmy Bolling's room?" When we said it was, from behind his back he pulled a huge, bright red fire truck and handed it to our big-eyed brother. Timmy said, "I've been waiting for you." As we cried and thanked him, we asked the kind doctor how he knew Timmy wanted a fire truck. He just grinned and went on his way.

After he was gone, we asked everyone we knew in the hospital who this man was and where he had gone. But nobody knew him—except Timmy. He said, "That was Jesus."

Can you imagine what feelings we had? We cried and laughed and cried some more. Timmy went on playing with his fire truck and didn't pay any attention to us. As far as he was concerned, we were all being silly. He had known all along that Jesus would bring him that shiny, red fire truck.

BY LINDA WORLEY

The Littlest Angel

❦   ❦   ❦

*S*IX MONTHS AT OUR CHURCH and young Denise still didn't seem to fit. It wasn't because of a lack of energy or a willingness to play. And it wasn't that she thought of herself as better than the rest, or that she was too shy or reserved. She was just as smart and active as the other eight-year-olds, but her height and weight were far below average—a by-product of having been undernourished and abandoned by her parents.

She and her three younger siblings had been found in a house with shabby furniture, no electricity, no water, and very little food. Despite the difficult circumstances, Denise had made sure that her brothers ate and felt what comfort she could provide—even when it meant giving up her own comfort.

A pair of social workers who belonged to our church had found the children. They arranged for one couple in the congregation to take the children into their home so that Denise and her brothers could stay together; several other families were helping to provide for the children. My wife and I watched them during the Sunday morning worship service while their foster parents played instruments in the church orchestra.

It was the holiday season and time for the annual Christmas pageant put on by the youth. Each year three girls were selected to be angels, wearing golden robes and wings. The angels knelt by the manger while all the members of our church walked by and paid homage. Ten minutes before the program, two of

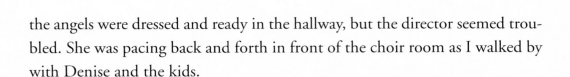

the angels were dressed and ready in the hallway, but the director seemed troubled. She was pacing back and forth in front of the choir room as I walked by with Denise and the kids.

"What's the matter?" I asked.

"The play's about to start, and I'm missing an angel," she said with a worried frown. Suddenly she noticed Denise and perked up as if her prayers were answered. "Can Denise be our angel?"

Knowing she was in a bind and that Denise was overjoyed, I consented.

Denise walked into the choir room beaming. I could tell that being an angel was very special to her. As I sat in my pew, waiting for the pageant to start, I began thinking about how Denise truly deserved the honor. Only an angel would act as a mother to three small children when she was just a child herself. Only an angel would give shelter to someone when she needed to be sheltered. Only an angel would sacrifice food and safety and love and tenderness when the same were in short supply to her.

The play started, and in a few minutes Denise practically floated onto the stage, truly looking the part. I looked down at her brothers, and each of them was bursting with happiness. It seemed to be just what they needed, seeing their sister on stage.

Later in the program, as we passed by the manger, Denise's face seemed to be glowing with pride. When we got back to our pews, the youngest of the brothers leaned close to me and whispered in my ear, "I think Denise makes a good angel, don't you?"

I smiled and said, "Yes, I do. She has certainly earned her wings."

BY HARRISON KELLY

Corey's Wings

COREY IS ONE OF THE six-year-olds in our small rural church. He has blue eyes, blond curls, pink cheeks, and a loud, hoarse voice. And he loves music. The doctors have already placed many labels on him, including developmentally disabled and autistic. But to those of us who know him, he is just "Our Corey." He wants so much to do what all the other children do.

At our Christmas Eve service, each class has a presentation. Last year, when it was time for all of the five-year-olds to perform, the youngsters stood up, marched down the long aisle, and formed a straight line across the front of the sanctuary. Corey slowly trudged along behind his other friends. Pinned to the back of each child's shirt were white, cardboard angel wings, outlined in old garland. A golden halo adorned each little head.

The whole class waited for Corey to get to the front. It seemed to take forever. He finally made his way up the three small steps and, of course, stood right in the center of the group. Then he walked over to check out the Christmas tree. Next he spotted his grandma and grandpa in a row near the back. He broke into a big, wide smile and waved his

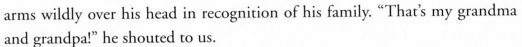

arms wildly over his head in recognition of his family. "That's my grandma and grandpa!" he shouted to us.

The class sang one of my favorites, "The Little Drummer Boy." Each child had been given a small drum and sticks. Corey kept gazing over the audience, seemingly oblivious to the song that had started. But then the "romp-pa-pom-poms" caught his attention. The second the other children finished a "romp-pa-pom-pom" with their drumsticks, Corey came in loud and clear with his own. It repeated over and over. Corey's beats were always an echo behind those of the other children. I smiled to myself as the words "marching to his own drumbeat" flitted through my mind.

The children performed the whole song. And right to the end, Corey was continually an echo behind the others. So when the children were finished, Corey still had his last "romp-pa-pom-pom" to do—his very own solo!

The other children marched back to their seats while Corey stood alone on the stage—in the spotlight. His blue eyes became even wider in wonderment as he once again looked around at the tree and then focused on the audience. He looked straight at Grandma and Grandpa. "I did it! I did it!" he exclaimed in disbelief.

Corey slowly made his way back down the steps and lumbered to his pew with the other children. As he walked past me, I felt the air softly move. I knew it must have been the brush of angel wings—and not just the cardboard ones pinned to the back of Corey's shirt.

BY ELAINE SLATER REESE

A Warm and Fuzzy Present

❦   ❦   ❦

My husband, Jim, and I have always been blessed with a house full of cats. Over the years, we've shared our home with 11 feline friends, all of whom were strays or from an animal shelter. And we always run an "outdoor café" on our porch to feed countless other strays. Weenie, our oldest and dearest cat, died in the fall of 1996, an especially painful time for us because I had recently suffered the loss of my entire family. Over a period of 11 months, my mother, father, and brother had all died of cancer. I was becoming increasingly depressed and could not bear the thought of the normally joyous holiday season without my family.

My downward slide became apparent at work, especially to a dear young man named Patrick. He and I had formed a close bond immediately after I started my job. His great sense of humor had instantly drawn me to him. He reminded me a great deal of my brother. I was also one of the few people who could see through the comedian on the outside to find the hurting teenager on the inside, crying out for attention and understanding. We were both from broken homes and had an overwhelming need to be loved. Perhaps that is what had really drawn me to him—in many ways, I understood his pain. It disturbed him to see me so depressed, especially at Christmastime. Knowing of my great affection for cats, and how much the recent loss of Weenie had added to my depression, Patrick decided to take action.

Whispers from Heaven ❦ **163**

He had heard about a poor little kitten that had been left to die, but miraculously someone had heard her faint cries and rescued her. She was taken to a local veterinary clinic, where she was first fed through an eyedropper and then eventually raised on a baby bottle. She spent the first three months of her life in the clinic, receiving constant love and attention from the staff. Patrick chose the perfect "mama" for this special kitten.

On December 23, he called me in to the kitchen at work and gave me a handsomely wrapped package. Immediately being suspicious of a prank, I shook it. The familiar sound of a box of cat food rattled through the kitchen. Everyone who had gathered started laughing, so I went along with Patrick's joke. I ripped off the paper and was holding a box of Kitten Chow. By this time, I was laughing, too, and thanked him. "Well, at least it's something I can always use!" At that moment, he took me by the hand and led me around the corner. There stood another coworker holding the most adorable little kitten I had ever seen! I was so shocked and surprised. I couldn't believe how kind and thoughtful my young friend had been. There aren't many people who would go to such lengths to give such a meaningful gift.

Patrick looked at me and said, "I figured this was the one thing you needed to cheer you up and help you make it through this Christmas." I was laughing and crying and hugging him at the same time. For once in my life, I was speechless!

As I walked closer to the kitten, our eyes met. There was an instant attraction, and I knew in my heart she was meant for me. She scrambled into my arms and crawled up the front of my Christmas Cat sweatshirt until her little head was resting on my right shoulder. It was there that she stayed for the rest of the afternoon, purring contentedly. Others tried to take her from me, but she held on to me for dear life. She had adopted me. I named her Angel, and everyone agreed it was the perfect name for this tiny gift from God—and, of course, Patrick.

I took Angel home and introduced her to her new brothers and sisters and my stunned but pleased husband. There was no period of adjustment as there had been with the other cats. Angel walked around like she owned the place. It seemed so familiar to her, as if she had been there before. It was then that I realized God had shown her the way, and she had accepted her assignment.

During her first night at home, she wasn't satisfied to sleep in the cozy little bed we had carefully prepared for her downstairs. Instead, she followed me up the steps and took her place on my pillow. And she did the same thing every night afterward! She placed her paws around my head as if holding me safely and protecting me from the world. I began to sleep more soundly and peacefully than I had in a very long time.

As Angel grew, we needed to change the sleeping arrangements because I no longer had a place on my pillow for me! Now she sleeps right next to me, lengthwise with her head on the pillow nestled close to mine. This gives her close access to my face when she feels the need for hugs and kisses during the night. If I make the "mistake" of trying to roll over and face away from her, she is forced to get up and properly throw herself down again on the other side, letting me know of her displeasure at being disturbed.

Angel always seems to sense when I am having an especially bad day because she makes it a point to stay as close as possible to me and smother me with extra kisses. She and our God always give me the strength and courage I need to go on another day.

Patrick is always anxious to hear of her latest escapades and devilish behavior. She makes us both laugh, even more than we did before, and that is quite an accomplishment!

Because of God's love for me and the special friendship I have with Patrick, as well as the unconditional love and understanding from my husband, I have been able to recover from my tremendous losses and can once again enjoy life. I firmly believe that God sent me the best gift of all that Christmas, and he used Patrick as the deliveryman.

BY BARBARA SPOTTS

O, LITTLE TOWN OF BETHLEHEM

O, little town of Bethlehem,
How still we see thee lie,
Above thy deep and dreamless sleep,
The silent stars go by;
Yet in thy dark streets shineth
The everlasting Light;
The hopes and fears of all the years
Are met in thee tonight.

PHILLIP BROOKS (1835–1893)

Always an Angel

M Y SISTER'S NAME is Angel. She is 28, and for the second time she is fighting cancer. It is a brain tumor. Slowly, her world has turned inside out, short-circuiting her abilities and changing her life forever.

The holidays hold an overwhelming loneliness for those in the hospital. Determined to make a difference, my sister asked our family for a special present and we obliged, returning to the hospital with bundles of red roses. As I rode the elevator to her floor, I looked down at the bouquet of red roses in my arms and my eyes burned with tears. Her desire to help those around her remains unaffected by her cancer.

Angel often struggles down the hall, hoping to brighten the days of the other patients. Because her right side is now paralyzed, she needs a nurse or one of us to help her. She has no idea that one look at her has me in tears. She still sees only other people's needs. Her own suffering is very evident to us, but she doesn't see it that way.

What matters to her are the people in the rooms around her who are scared, lonely, in pain, and hopeless. She understands what it means to wake up in the middle of the night in a strange hospital room, with strange people milling about, longing for home and a familiar bed.

Angel actually thanks God in her prayers for this challenge and opportunity. That is how she sees it—an opportunity. Her selflessness and compassion

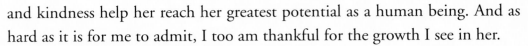

and kindness help her reach her greatest potential as a human being. And as hard as it is for me to admit, I too am thankful for the growth I see in her.

Giving to others makes Angel feel alive. Her smile lights up their rooms, and the instant the other patients see her, they feel the warmth of her love and genuine compassion. For many of them, Angel is their only visitor for days at a time. She waits for us to visit, or for a nurse to have a free moment, so that she can be wheeled to make her "rounds."

The elevator doors open, and I quickly brush the tears away and force my brightest smile for her. I breeze into her room with her Christmas roses held toward her.

Grinning into her blue eyes, the same shade as mine, I help her into the wheelchair and watch in wonder as she carefully separates each rose with her left hand. Angel and I then slowly begin our trek to each room on the floor.

I watch the faces, full of pain, transform into radiant smiles as they see my sister. She has this way of bringing light and goodness, of touching hearts. She makes them forget, for just a few wonderful moments, that they are in a hospital. During their few moments with her, they feel the joy of Christmas, as good as gingerbread and softly falling snow. She brings Christmas joy into each room and leaves behind a lingering spirit of hope.

She tires as we finish our visits. Each patient has received a beautiful Christmas rose and a sense of being loved. She has become their Christmas Angel.

BY SUSAN FAHNCKE

The Kindness of a Stranger

"YOUR DAUGHTER IS SO concerned about you, it's starting to affect her schoolwork," my fourth-grader's teacher solemnly told me during a parent-teacher conference. "She's really worried about you." With a sense of guilt and shame, I realized that my personal problems were having a damaging effect on my youngest child, Mary.

I was embarrassed that the teacher now knew about my personal difficulties through my child. I mumbled apologetically that my 70-year-old mother had died suddenly only weeks before from a stroke. I explained that although I had been depressed over her death, I never dreamed that nine-year-old Mary had been so perceptive of my pain.

Quickly thinking back, I remembered the breakfast in bed that Mary had served me the week before. Bringing dry toast and canned juice to me was her way of trying to lift my spirits. But I had been too depressed to realize her deep concern, even though I'd been touched by getting breakfast in bed—a luxury I'd never received before, not even on Mother's Day.

Now it was only three weeks to Christmas, and I couldn't get into the spirit of the season. I hadn't baked any

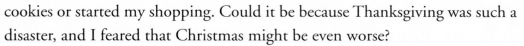

cookies or started my shopping. Could it be because Thanksgiving was such a disaster, and I feared that Christmas might be even worse?

With a heavy heart, I had prepared and served the traditional Thanksgiving dinner for my husband, our four children, and my widowed father. We all felt something was missing—my mother. I tried to be cheerful, especially to help my elderly father get through the day. I held up fairly well until it was time to wash the dishes and put them away. Then I started crying because the after-dinner clean-up had always been a special time for Mother and me. We would talk and share many things as we worked side by side in the kitchen.

Now Mother was gone, and I felt as if I couldn't carry on the usual Christmas celebration without her. I needed her! I secretly wished we could skip Christmas this year. I just didn't have the energy for it.

My husband put up a beautiful lighted nativity scene outdoors. The children helped decorate the house, and everything looked lovely, but I still could not overcome my deep sense of loss. Mother had always been an essential part of our Christmas festivities, and now she wasn't around to share in the preparations. During this holiday season, I wanted her advice and assistance on everything from making and wrapping gifts for the children to baking such traditional treats as Bohemian *kolaches,* a fruit-filled pastry my family loves.

My husband insisted that he take me shopping to select a new Christmas outfit. He thought new clothes might cheer me up. I protested that I didn't need anything. "I have several really nice dresses," I told him. But he persisted. "Wouldn't you like to have something new to wear to Christmas parties?" I told him emphatically that I didn't want to go to any Christmas parties. I explained that I preferred to be left alone in my grief.

Finally, I consented to go shopping with him. After looking numbly through racks of clothes, I chose a white linen outfit. Looking back, I think I selected white over the usual bright colors that I love because I felt so colorless and empty. I brought the outfit home and hung it in the closet, still not feeling any joy—only guilt for not being excited about my new clothes.

At a church potluck one night, I confided to another woman that I was having trouble getting into the spirit of Christmas this year since my mother had passed away only a few weeks earlier. "It's so hard. I just can't find any joy in the season," I told her sadly, admitting my wish to forgo Christmas entirely.

After listening sympathetically, the woman tried to console me, and she encouraged me to get into the holiday spirit for the sake of my family. But even her kind words didn't help. As Christmas drew nearer, I became even more depressed. I forced myself to buy and wrap some gifts for my husband, my father, and my children. I can't remember now what I bought, but I didn't put much thought or love into the gifts. I did bake a few simple sugar cookies, but I didn't decorate them, and I couldn't bring myself to make the usual fancy holiday goodies. "These cookies will just have to do," I sighed.

Two days before Christmas, the lady who had so lovingly listened to my troubles at the church dinner called me at home. She told me that she had made an extra dish of the Mexican casserole I had liked so much at the church potluck, and she asked if she could bring it over to me while it was still hot.

As I waited for her to arrive, I decided to step outside into the cool night air. I stared at the dark nativity scene, shivering and alone, with the wind blowing through me. Then I turned on the lights. The radiant warmth of the scene made my heart swell, and a lump formed in my throat. *This is what Christmas is really about,* I thought. *God gave his best to us—his only son at Christmas—and now a new friend is giving her best to me.*

When the woman arrived, I greeted her cheerfully. We stood in front of the lighted Bethlehem scene, reflecting on the age-old story of the first Christmas. Awkwardly, she held the hot casserole out as her "offering" to me as a friend and fellow Christian.

"I wanted to give you something…because…you're just you," she stammered, slightly embarrassed, not knowing how to explain her unexpected gift from the heart. I smiled and thanked her, thinking what a beautiful compliment she had just given me.

I looked back at the nativity scene and gave thanks in my heart to God for my Christmas angel friend. With her heartfelt gifts of food and friendship, she seemed to me like an angel coming to proclaim the Good News of Christmas. Her generous, caring holiday spirit pushed away the depression I had been fighting for weeks and ushered in the true loving spirit of the season. Thanks to my Christmas angel friend, I was able to celebrate the birthday of Jesus with joy and peace in my heart.

BY MARGARET MALSAM

Selfishness makes Christmas a burden: love makes it a delight.

ANONYMOUS

My Christmas Angel

❦   ❦   ❦

ON A COLD DECEMBER DAY in 1997, my youngest son and I set out to finish some last-minute Christmas shopping. This wasn't the joyous holiday shopping that most imagine. The holidays had lost all joy since the day my second-eldest son died.

Getting through the season was just the object of the game. Every present and every ornament just accentuated the absence and emptiness my family felt. One more Christmas was just one more Christmas without him.

This Christmas, however, was to be different. This Christmas would be a step forward.

When entering a clothing store, my son, Lance, and I headed in separate directions. I headed for a chenille scarf, beige and soft, a sense of comfort. I liked how it felt, the soft, furry feeling flowing through my grasp. All things seemed beige for me: lacking of color, lacking that richness of life, reminding me of my loneliness.

Suddenly, I was interrupted. Not a bad interruption, though. It was a sweet, smiling, happy teenager. You know the kind. The one who has no cares, not even for the paycheck, who just likes to get out and enjoy life. His smile brought one to mine.

The young man asked if I had seen his friend, Bob, a sweater-adorned teddy bear that he was holding in his arms. He informed me that his earlier friend, Billy, was purchased a short time ago, and that more bears were for sale at the register.

It was then I realized that they were strategically placed at locations around the store for all to see. If the youngster hadn't said anything, I wouldn't have noticed. My vision was tunneled: Get in and get out.

I decided to buy the chenille scarf for my mother. Meanwhile, my son searched through mounds of the usual Christmas-fair sweaters. We rummaged through to find a size for him and headed for the register.

The joy of the boyish smile on the salesclerk persuaded me to treat myself a little, to find comfort in a bear of my own. When I said I wanted to purchase a bear, my son gave me the usual "are you kidding me?" smile and chuckled. I knew for him this was a happy thing, though. It was a chance for me to let just a little of the Scrooge in me go and enjoy a touch of Christmas.

When the girl turned to the shelves adorned with lonely bears behind her, she asked if I wanted one with a green or blue sweater. When I said green, she snatched one from the mass and plopped him down on the counter.

Just before she rang him up, a shout from a sales-girl stopped her cold. The girl quickly gave her the bear she had hidden behind the counter, obviously the one she had adopted as her own. "No, take this one," she said. "He needs a good home. I have been taking care of him." The girl at the register turned to seek my approval, and I nodded. It seemed fitting and sweet, as if I were really taking care of him for her. They packed the bear in a bag, and I paid for the gifts.

My son and I headed back into the mall for more heartbreaking joy. Lance turned to me with a sad and solemn look. "You didn't hear the bear's name, did you?" he asked. "What do you, mean?" I replied. He told me to look on the sweater at his name.

As I reached in the bag, I pulled out the sweet, innocent friend I had adopted and found the tag safely pinned to his chest. I read the simply typed name: "Timothy." A feeling of total emptiness flowed from my heart through my entire body. *No, it couldn't be*, I thought. Not the name of all my emotions. Not the name that has been attached to every feeling of happiness, sorrow, and definitely pain. The name of my lost son.

As tears ran down my face, I knew this wasn't to be sad. This was his sign. This was Tim telling me that no matter what, no matter when, he would always be there. Tim wasn't gone to a place without me. Not gone into oblivion, not frolicking in a field of clover never knowing of our life together. He was watching, loving, and protecting me.

This wasn't the end of the pain—that would never be. But it did bring joy. It did bring me comfort knowing he was in heaven and with me.

He was a child of God, present and accounted for. I grabbed my bear and my son and felt the joy and pain of his closeness.

Timothy is, and always will be, my Christmas angel.

BY KATHERINE ERWIN

The Season of Love

Blessed is the season which engages the whole world in a conspiracy of love.

Hamilton Wright Mable

Keeping the Harvest

❦ ❦ ❦

HE SKIRTED THE BEND where a few cornstalks still stood, stout sentinels of the garden patch. Late afternoon sunlight filtered through a canopy of naked cottonwoods, lacing the ground with gray shadows. Underfoot, the music of December crunched in dry leaves.

It was the season for "after harvest"—or what Emma had called their "time of plenty." A time to count their many blessings. Long after the last sun-ripened tomato had been picked, the last of the autumn raspberries eaten, and the garden put to bed for the winter, his wife always insisted on seeking out other gifts of nature.

Fred knew the best places to start. After all, he had searched and gathered on every square foot of this property for 44 years now. Planted it. Tended it.

If Emma were here....

But Emma wasn't here. So he would do alone what they had always rejoiced in doing together.

At the grape arbor, Fred took out his pocketknife and slashed at aged vines, careful to cut away only the overgrowth. When he determined he had enough, his calloused hands shaped the supple veins to form a wreath.

At the edge of his pond, Fred combed through the disheveled heads of cat-tails. Finding two still nappy and whole, he snapped them from their stalks and laced them through one side of the wreath.

At the fence line, Fred clipped a few twigs of juniper berries and harvested two feathery plumes from the towering pampas grass. Thick fingers knew automatically where to put them, how to secure them.

He paused beneath the mountain ash. Bending low, he reached cautiously among the holly bushes for spiny leaves and glossy crimson berries. They would add a festive touch. Satisfied, he passed the wreath carefully through both hands, inspecting it for soundness, for balance, for beauty.

The drive to Columbine's Alzheimer Unit was short and pleasant. Humming under his breath, Fred nodded a greeting at the nurses' station and walked into the day room.

Emma stared unseeingly out the bank of windows while her vein-ridged hand plucked repetitively at the hem of her blouse. Fred laid his offering on a table and leaned to kiss his wife.

"Look what I made today, Sweetheart, to hang on your door." Fred pointed to the wreath. "It's 'after harvest,' and the property is brimming with all your favorite things—everything you like to gather to celebrate the season."

Bleached blue eyes focused on Fred's gift.

"See how thick and sound the grapevines are now, Emma? Remember how you insisted we plant those spindly things the very first year we moved to the farm?" Stilling her twitching hand with his own, he guided it around the broad circle.

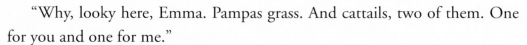

"Why, looky here, Emma. Pampas grass. And cattails, two of them. One for you and one for me."

Her tentative finger traced the velvety lengths.

"And, oh, Honey, these beauties are clustered thick beneath mountain ash. Nearly had to fight off the grackles to get to the holly this year! You should've heard them scolding me from the branches. Do you remember the Christmas that..."

Emma was smiling. Fred squeezed her hand and grinned back.

If she couldn't tromp through the seasons herself, then he would bring those blessings to her. After all, it was a "time of plenty"—plenty of memories. And Fred had gathered enough for the both of them.

BY CAROL MCADOO REHME

It is Christmas in the mansion,
Yule-log fires and silken frocks.
It is Christmas in the cottage,
Mother's filling little socks.
It is Christmas on the highway,
In the thronging, busy mart.
But the dearest, truest Christmas
Is the Christmas in the heart.
—AUTHOR UNKNOWN

Christmas With Dad

*I*T HAD BEEN 25 YEARS since I last spent Christmas with my father. I had been a small girl when our family had our final Christmas together, and the memories had washed away over the years. In fact, I could no longer remember ever waking up to see my dad on Christmas morning. And now a generation later, he was here to spend the holidays with my own family.

His Christmas stocking hung on the mantle next to ours, the name "Papa" at the top, and I looked at it with pride. My dad for Christmas. I didn't realize how much I missed it until now. Ironically, our roles were now reversed. With children of my own, I was playing Santa for him. I couldn't wait to see his face, watching his grandchildren's faces on our first Christmas morning together. I knew it was a gift to us all.

I happily shopped for and wrapped his presents with love and eager excitement. For the first time in many years, I didn't have to mail them. The children each chose presents for their papa, and they were as excited as I was to spend their first Christmas with their grandfather. It was a time of getting to know him and he us.

During the week before Christmas, we filled our days with baking and holiday music. My father and my husband got to know each other, as they worked on projects around the house. It was wonderful to hear them working together, hammering and painting, while talking about family.

We had family time together each night, my father joining us in prayer and scripture reading. I knew he had no one to pray with, and I often saw tears trickle down his cheeks as he felt the Lord's love in our home. How the years of being alone must have taken their toll! I couldn't imagine spending as many holidays as he did alone, and although I know it was by choice, he must have felt a deep loneliness, especially at Christmastime. He hadn't known what it meant to have a complete family for years, and I began to imagine for the first time what that must have been like for him.

Dad took my teenage son for walks, their relationship bonding in the crisp frosty air, under the street lamps and snow flurries. He spent time coloring with my youngest daughter, discussing the meaning of life as they tried to stay between the lines. Our three-year-old and 14-year-old, for the first time ever, got to spend their birthdays with Papa, as both were during the Christmas season. The three-year-old played endless hours of trains with him, and occasionally I had to break up an argument over whose turn it was to drive the train. They wrestled and laughed, and I watched my father grow as a man during the time spent with my children.

Our relationship also grew, and I was grateful. We sang Christmas carols together, with his smooth voice rekindling childhood memories of him playing the guitar and my sisters and I singing along with him. The good memories began to resurface, and I felt that an emptiness that I had never realized was there was being filled by my father's presence.

Christmas morning arrived. I was up before the children, sleepy-eyed and in my nightgown, grasping the video camera and waiting for my family to wake up, afraid to miss a moment of it. Curled up on the couch in the dark, camera in hand, I suddenly remembered a Christmas with my dad—our last one together. I smiled as the warmth of the memory came over me: My father's laugh and the squeals from my sisters seemed to fill the room again. It was a small moment, frozen in time, but a gift for me nevertheless. The twinkling of the lights on our Christmas tree kept me company as I reflected on Christmases past and present.

The children finally woke up, and my bleary-eyed father stumbled down the stairs to join the melee. Handing the camera to my husband, I hugged my dad and handed him his Christmas stocking, crammed with surprises for him. "Merry Christmas, Daddy." Tears slowly made their way down my father's face, and he held me tighter than he ever had. Through the tears, he whispered, "Merry Christmas, honey. I love you." I knew we had come full-circle and that time had given me a gift I had waited a quarter of a century to receive.

BY SUSAN FAHNCKE

To Grandmother's House We Go

❧   ❧   ❧

*T*HERE WE WERE, Christmas on wheels, loading up, ready to go. It never made any sense to me, growing up, why we did it every Christmas. We'd get up super early, cook until we collapsed, then pack up bowls, trays, platters, and just about everything in sight to haul across the bridge an hour away to my grandparents' house.

Sure, it sounds wonderful, the holiday shared with loved ones, the entire family together for a warm, special, close time. That's the way it sounds. But in reality, it didn't work out that way. In reality, it was all struggle. Just think of the amount of clear wrap and aluminum foil we used in a single day. It was staggering. And we all worked like squirrels storing nuts for the winter. I wore an apron wrapped around me and got just as hot and steamy as my mother always did.

Most years, I thought I'd never want to catch sight of a crisp, nicely browned, steamy turkey again as long as I lived, not after helping defrost the hapless bird, empty stuff from its insides, slather butter all over the thing, shove it into the oven, then keep watch over it for hours. Being a picky eater myself, I never quite got excited about spending days cooking a feast that would be devoured in a matter of minutes.

Everything had to be cooked to within an inch of its life—but not too far gone. It would all have to withstand the hour-long trip without disintegrating, then undoubtedly face warming up once we got there. We mashed potatoes, baked pies, tore up bread for homemade stuffing, shelled walnuts, scraped vegetables, and on and on.

Do I sound selfish? Perhaps, but I haven't even mentioned the half of it. We went through all this anguish over the feast that my great-grandmother would look at, hands on hips, and proclaim in a firm voice: "All that food just for us? What a waste. We won't eat a fraction of it. We don't need all that." Then she'd march off to the pantry, perch on a high stool, and consume butter bread with sugar sprinkled on top.

My grandmother would fuss about how to fit it all on the table, whether it was hot enough, whether anybody would like the sweet potatoes done that way, and whether the mashed potatoes were lumpy again. My grandfather would grunt, mumble words no one deciphered, grumble about having to move around so many chairs and open the table wider, and then evaluate how unevenly Dad sliced the turkey.

Every year the same. All that hard work to bring our Christmas to share with them. Then the long drive, all the setting up, all the packing up again, and for what? Nobody seemed pleased to see us. We caused a whole lot of fuss and trouble, it seemed to me. I always suspected my grandparents would be happier left to themselves, settled in their favorite chairs, watching their usual TV shows or complaining when specials bumped their regulars off the air.

I had decided years ago that bringing Christmas to their house annoyed them more than anything else. We always burst in, full of holiday cheer and good wishes, noisy, pink-cheeked from the cold, bumping things, almost knocking over the collections of figurines covering every available surface. We came loaded down with gaily wrapped gifts that they always told us we should not have bought.

"Why waste money buying us gifts?" they'd ask, holding up the latest flannel shirt or colorful sweater. "You don't need to do this. We've got everything we need." Then they'd tuck the gifts back into their boxes, pack them away in drawers, and leave them there for a decade or two.

So, why bother? I asked Mom that often when I was younger and full of sass. "Mom, why do we do this? They don't like anything we do."

"Hush," Mom would tell me. "They're your grandparents. We do it to show how much we love them."

"Couldn't we just mail presents and call them?"

Mom glared. "This is family. This is what family does." And that was that. No more arguments. No logic. No commonsense. No hope of a quiet, peaceful, lazy Christmas at home, just us, enjoying our gifts and tree, our own comfortable fireplace, our own roomy dining table, our own stuff, which wasn't as fragile as the stuff at our grandparents' house. Nobody minded us knocking things over in our own house; most of our stuff bounced and came out just fine.

So, year after year we trekked across that bridge, loaded down with gifts nobody wanted and food nobody liked. Year after year we listened to murmurs and mumbling about our lumpy potatoes or overspending on gifts. But . . . then came the year I finally understood what this was all about, the year that opened my eyes, the year that made all the others make sense.

It was a special year, a year in which we had some setbacks ourselves—wage cutbacks, that sort of thing. Not our easiest year. Mom was weary. I could see it in her face, hear it in her voice. But she was stubborn, insisting we go on same as ever, making sure we took the best and brightest Christmas possible to our grandparents.

We did all our regular stuff. Then we packed the car and headed across the bridge toward our destination. We arrived as usual and were greeted with the typical fuss. "Don't shake snow on the carpet. . . . Be careful not to spill that gravy. . . . You could feed three armies with all that food."

It was later, after dinner, after the cleaning up, that I caught my grandfather in a quiet, private moment, a moment I wasn't meant to see. He held his best gift in both hands—a collage frame, with photos of each of his grandchildren. His usually gruff expression had softened. His eyes seemed shiny, and I caught sight of a tear sliding down his leathery cheek. He half smiled, something he didn't do often, at least where we could catch him at it.

And suddenly I understood. I knew in that moment that all this trouble and fuss did mean something to my grandparents, though they wouldn't let it show, though they didn't want us to catch them in a sentimental moment. I don't know why. Maybe they weren't comfortable showing much emotion. Maybe they were embarrassed by tears. Maybe they felt more at ease with complaints.

But I knew in that instant that we mattered to them, that our gifts mattered, that all the hard work and effort every year mattered. They cared. I felt it to my very core. I tiptoed away, leaving my grandfather to his privacy. When we left that night, I kissed his rough cheek and hugged him tightly. He grunted, nodded, turned halfway aside. But I knew what I knew, and I would never begrudge those Christmases on wheels again.

BY KAREN M. LEET

THE SEASON OF LOVE

Living Up to Martha Stewart

❦ ❦ ❦

MARRYING INTO SOMEONE else's family is never easy. For Maddie, that was an understatement. She had not only married a man who had been embroiled in a bitter divorce up until two years ago, but she also married his two teenage daughters, both of whom blamed Maddie for their parents' breakup.

In fact, Maddie had not even met Roger until long after his divorce was final. They had not lived together, and Maddie had only moved in with Roger the day after their wedding, skipping the honeymoon until after the holidays. She did understand that his daughters needed a scapegoat. Still, it would not make her first Christmas with Jennifer and Brittany any easier, especially since they were upset about not getting to spend the holidays with their mother this year. Roger had insisted upon it. To make matters worse, Maddie had agreed to make Christmas dinner, in a kitchen that was as foreign to her as her new stepchildren.

Roger was a supportive husband, and a loving father, and he did his best to try and bring the three women together. They had attempted some awkward dinners out on the town together, where basically Roger and Maddie spent the whole night trying to get the girls to drop the silent treatment, with little success. Maddie knew she had to get over this hump in order to try and make their new family work.

188 ❧ *Whispers from Heaven*

She decided to do much of the Christmas Day dinner preparations on Christmas Eve day, while Roger took the two girls out for some last-minute shopping. It gave Maddie some breathing room, having a day to herself to get used to the kitchen she had only been introduced to a few days prior. She had bought all the fixings for a big turkey dinner with all the trimmings, and she wanted everything to be perfect.

Maddie had it all planned out. She would bake and cook everything but the turkey on Christmas Eve day. She would make mashed potatoes, sweet potatoes, pumpkin pie, cherry pie, and her famous onion/green bean casserole. By the time she would finish, only the turkey itself would need to be baked. Everything else would just require a quick heating up. She had always loved to cook, and she idolized Martha Stewart. Although she was no gourmet chef, this was one dinner menu she was sure she could ace.

But the universe had other plans for Maddie. First the oven wouldn't heat up enough, then it seemed to get way too hot for its settings. Maddie burnt the cherry pie to a crisp. Moreover, she had been so embroiled in making the green bean casserole that she didn't realize until later that she had forgotten to buy the onions. She ran back to the store before they closed for Christmas Eve. She got back to the house only to realize that she had also forgotten the whipping cream for the pumpkin pie. There would be no whipping cream.

Things proceeded to go from not-so-good to bad to worse. She dropped the entire plate of mashed potatoes onto the tile floor, sending shards of glass and potato globs everywhere. There would be no mashed potatoes. As she struggled to clean up that mess before Roger and the girls got home, the oven started smoking, setting off the fire alarm. Maddie sat on the floor in a state of

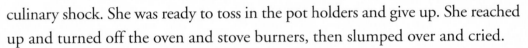

culinary shock. She was ready to toss in the pot holders and give up. She reached up and turned off the oven and stove burners, then slumped over and cried.

That's how Roger and the girls found her a half-hour later when they came home. Maddie was so embarrassed that she didn't say a word as she ran past them and into the bedroom, closing the door as if to close off the rest of the world. She fell on the bed in tears, sure she had made a complete fool of herself in front of the girls she so desperately wanted to impress. Roger came in and tried to console her, but she was beyond consolation. He asked her to come back downstairs to enjoy some eggnog, but Maddie begged off, wanting only to go to sleep and forget that the day had ever happened.

Roger kissed her and went downstairs. Jennifer and Brittany were on their way out the door. He asked where they were going, but they just smiled and said, "To do some damage control." Roger shook his head, wondering what they meant, only to find out when they returned over an hour later, armed to the teeth with groceries from a nearby 24-hour market. He watched, his heart swelling with pride and gratitude, as the girls took over the kitchen and set about repairing Maddie's destroyed dinner plans. They followed Maddie's menu, remaking the mashed potatoes, the pie, the sweet potatoes, and the casserole.

Well into the night, they worked like culinary elves, their smiles growing bigger. Roger stayed up with them, and they talked as they had never done before, about the divorce and their bitterness toward Maddie. Roger explained that Maddie only wanted to be their friend, not a replacement for their mother. He tried to convince them to stop blaming Maddie for what had happened between him and their mother, and he assured them that Maddie made him happier than he had been in a long time.

The girls opened up about their own angers and fears and uncertainties about Maddie. But Roger saw through their resistance, realizing that they, too, wanted to like and be accepted by Maddie. Otherwise, they would not be spending their Christmas Eve doing what they were doing.

On Christmas morning, Maddie woke up late—to her distress. She quickly washed up and changed, wondering if she could possibly salvage any of her dinner plans in time. When she walked downstairs and into the kitchen, Roger passed her in the hallway and gave her a big kiss on the cheek. He was smiling from ear to ear. Maddie wondered what was up.

She entered the kitchen to find Jennifer and Brittany already dressed and busy cooking up a storm. Maddie stopped in her tracks, her mouth open, as she noticed her own handwritten menu displayed where the two girls could follow it. As she stood there, dumbfounded, Jennifer smiled at her and said, "C'mon over and chop some onions!" It took a moment for Maddie to respond, but she did so with fresh tears and a big smile—of relief and joy. Brittany grabbed Maddie by the hand, dragging her to the counter. "The sweet potatoes really, really need you!"

The three of them managed to salvage Maddie's dinner. When they all sat down to eat with Roger, instead of the silent treatment, there was a lot of eating and talking and laughing over the best Christmas dinner Maddie had ever had.

After dinner, the girls carried the pies into the dining room—along with the whipped cream. Maddie realized that she had received a very special gift that day—the gift of acceptance from her new family.

As Martha Stewart would say, it was a "good thing."

BY MARIE JONES

Broken Cookies

❧ ❧ ❧

BAKING SEASONAL TREATS to donate and deliver to area families was a Christmas tradition for the Gardners. It was also an exercise in cooperation when Mother marshaled all eight children into the kitchen one December evening.

"Laura, I'm putting you in charge of both the cookie batter and the twins. Here is the recipe. Here are the twins."

"Ruth, I think you can manage to find sprinkles, red hots, and chocolate chips to decorate with."

"Boys, come with me and I'll teach you the art of making your granny's special frosting."

As the six-year-old family caboose, Bessie was dubbed "Jill-of-all-trades" and ended up being the official helper. Everyone's helper. Oh, how she loved helping. She helped Laura and the twins. "Bessie, I know Daddy likes crispy cookies, but get those eggshells out of my batter!"

She helped Ruth. "Uh-uh, Bessie. Absolutely no rubber band halos on these angel cookies."

She helped Mother and the boys. "No, dear, I don't think eight cups of sugar is better than two."

As you might imagine, mixing, cutting, baking, and icing took them well into the night—in spite of all Bessie did to help. The final batch was Bessie's favorite—a dozen Rudolph the Red-nosed Reindeers. This year, she got to place the glowing red hots at the tips of their snouts!

Finally, the mixing bowls, spoons, and baking sheets (they used a lot of them) were washed and put away. All of the flat surfaces (and, yes, that included the floor) were wiped clean of spills. All of the cookies were cut and decorated (with a serious attention to detail genetically programmed into each of the children), then set aside. Mother dug out her giant Tupperware bowls.

Gingerly, each sweet treat was lifted. Proudly, each work of art was admired. Not a star was chipped; not a halo cracked. After they filled and stacked three huge containers, Bessie grabbed the last lid, stretched all the way across the kitchen counter to help, and . . .

Down came the bowls, cookies and all.

Talk about "Silent Night." Everyone stared at the floor. Everyone stared at each other. Then everyone looked at Bessie. Nobody said a word—at least for a minute—which was exactly enough time for Bessie to race to her bedroom and bury her head under a pillow.

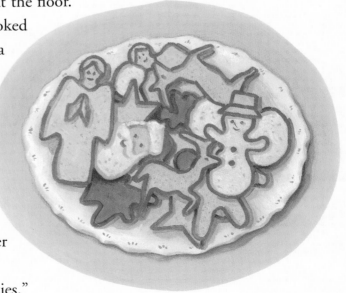

Then, through her sobs and her heart-break, she heard it: Mother's crooning as she rubbed Bessie's back. At last, Bessie quieted enough to listen. Only she didn't hear the lecture she felt she deserved and expected from her tired, disappointed parent.

"Don't cry," Mother said. "They're only cookies."

Gathering the little girl in her arms, Mother brushed back matted bangs, tucked Bessie's silky-blond head under her chin, and began to hum again as she rocked back and forth. She started to chuckle.

Suspiciously, Bessie pulled back and looked up, right into her mother's smiling face.

"Are you laughing?"

"Yes," said Mother. "I certainly am. After all, 25 years from now we'll be laughing about this anyway. So why wait? Why don't you and I just go ahead and laugh now?"

"Now?"

"Now."

Bessie smiled through her tears. At the moment, nothing was more important than her bruised little-girl heart. Not the mess, not the cookies, not the others.

A lot of Christmases have come and gone since then. So many, in fact, that this Christmas Bessie and her own little helper will follow family tradition and bake holiday cookies to donate and deliver. But the memory of that particular Christmas doesn't dim with time. It only gets brighter. You could even say it glows.

BY CAROL McADOO REHME

A Cherished Past, A Hopeful Present

STANDING ONLY TWO FEET TALL, it wasn't much of a tree. It was decorated only with a popcorn strand and a tin-foil star on top; it was all they could afford.

With his new assignment, Neil and his young wife, Jan, found themselves alone in a foreign country. Nevertheless, the delight of their first year together made the spirit of Christmas even more special than ever, allowing them time to reflect upon the true meaning of the season.

As they sat together beside the little tree on Christmas Eve, they took turns reading through the story of Jesus' birth from the book Jan's parents had sent them. It was a beautiful book—definitely the most expensive item they currently owned. Once finished, they decided to exchange their newspaper-wrapped gifts.

Neil picked his up first and handed it to Jan. She gently unwrapped it and found a pair of costume earrings inside. "They're beautiful," she said cheerfully as she clipped them on.

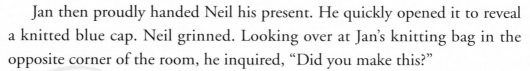

Jan then proudly handed Neil his present. He quickly opened it to reveal a knitted blue cap. Neil grinned. Looking over at Jan's knitting bag in the opposite corner of the room, he inquired, "Did you make this?"

She nodded her head, smiling proudly.

Neil was touched. The time and thought Jan had put into his gift made it worth far more than the price of its yarn.

"You're wonderful," he whispered, and he gave his new wife a kiss.

For the next several years, Neil wore the blue cap every winter, even after they could afford nicer ones. They eventually acquired a comfortable home and raised three children. For 25 years, they were blessed with deep-seeded love. Once the kids were grown, however, Jan was stricken with a serious disease. Although she fought it for several years, she ultimately lost her battle.

Shortly afterward, the family decided that it was time to remove Jan's belongings from the house. Neil wasn't sure he was ready yet, but he reluctantly agreed to it. He sat on the bed, watching his daughters rummaging through the closet and removing all of Jan's clothes.

Watch. That's all he could bring himself to do—and even that was extremely difficult. Sometimes they discovered something of his on Jan's side of the closet and promptly returned it to his side. At one point when they were almost finished, his oldest daughter came across the old knitted blue cap. She turned around, holding it toward him, and said, "I remember this. You wore it all the time when I was little."

Neil seized the cap with heartache. His eyes reddened and tears streamed relentlessly down his cheeks. His daughter sat down beside him, put her arm around his back, and rested her head on his shoulder.

"It's OK, Dad," she said. "It's only clothes. We're still keeping Mom in our hearts."

Neil looked down at the floor to hide his grief, but he nodded his acknowledgment.

"Hello. . . ." A voice called from the other room. It was Neil's mom, stopping by the house to cook dinner. Her mother came along as well. They all sat down together in the living room. Neil looked over at his grandmother. He contemplated how lucky he was that she was still around. Not only was she 97 years old, but she was still very witty. He sulkily contemplated how ironic it was that his wife hadn't outlived his grandmother. Jan should still be here; her life was short-changed and, therefore, so was his.

His grandma interrupted his brooding. "Neil, do you care if I have that knitting bag over there? It's not yours, is it?"

"No, you can have it."

Of course it wasn't his. The question was just a way to avoid mentioning that it had been Jan's and that she wouldn't need it anymore. Actually, he was surprised that his grandma wanted it. He didn't think her fingers were as operational as her intellect. However, he knew she had knitted frequently in her youth. Maybe she would get *some* use from it.

As he reached down to get it for her, he noticed several skeins of blue and cream yarn inside with about six inches of knitted rows resting on top. Jan had renewed her knitting hobby after becoming confined indoors. He recalled walking in on her unexpectedly one day and seeing her working with the blue yarn. She quickly put it away as if embarrassed. Unfortunately, she didn't finish whatever she had started, and now it would never be finished.

Neil handed the bag to his grandma, who looked happy and eager to take it. Apparently, it meant much more to her than he thought.

Neil wished he could be happy, yet even if he could he wouldn't. It wasn't right. How could he feel happiness when Jan was robbed of the same privilege?

Eventually it was time to face his first Christmas without Jan. Being together with the rest of the family was enjoyable, but it also made it extremely obvious that Jan was missing. He looked around at the decorations. His children had bought him a tree after realizing he wasn't going to. Then they got out the Christmas boxes and put up the familiar adornments. Although he didn't feel like celebrating, he respected their attempt to raise his spirits.

So everything was in its usual place just like every other year, but Jan's absence made the celebration awkward. They were doing things differently. Anything Jan had usually done had to be absorbed by someone else. It also took longer to get anything started, similar to the way activities are delayed when waiting for a late guest to arrive. Then the realization would sink in that everyone was already there.

After dinner it was time for presents. Neil wasn't in the mood for gifts, but he could tell that everyone had put more thought into them this Christmas—especially his. Instead of socks and cologne, he received pictures, concert tickets, a self-written poem, and a book about baseball, his favorite pastime.

Finally, the only gift left to open was the one from his grandma. It was soft and rectangular—probably a sweater. She usually didn't spend much, but she probably wanted to give him something special this year. He began tearing the paper off. His mood suddenly changed as he realized what was inside—a magnificent blue and cream afghan.

Neil held it up to appreciate it in its entirely, then asked his grandma in disbelief, "Did you make this?"

She nodded her head, smiling proudly.

"I didn't think you could."

"It wasn't easy. My eyesight's bad and my hands ache, but that little knitting bag caught my eye for a reason. It contained the beginning of an afghan I knew Jan was making for you. It's as much from her as it is from me, you know."

He did know. Jan began their life together with a knitted gift of love, and near the end of her life she had tried to make another loving gift for him. Even though she wasn't able to finish it herself, his grandma had somehow gotten the message to get the afghan ready for him by Christmas.

Neil brought the afghan to his face, caressing it. Jan's presence overcame him in a sweep of joy, and he could feel her smiling down on him at that very moment. From that point on, he knew he was going to be okay.

By Trista Linman

An angel of the Lord appeared to them, and
the glory of the Lord shone around them, and
they were so afraid. But the angel said to them
"Do not be afraid. I bring you good news of
great joy that will be for all the people."

Luke 2:9–10

Coconut Cake

IT WAS A THREE-LAYERED MASTERPIECE that seemed to rise like an ivory tower. It was a monument, a dream, simply unbeatable. My Aunt Elsie's coconut cake. There was only one in the whole wide world, and, when I was seven years old, it was the only want I had for Christmas.

That Christmas afternoon Aunt Elsie brought the delicate treasure to my house, and I savored every bite, letting each taste linger in my mouth, like each long, happy moment of a child's Christmas Day. It was even more memorable because it was my first Christmas in our family's new house. Before, we had lived in a two-story apartment building in the midtown section of Memphis.

As an energetic youngster, I prowled the halls of that apartment building as if they were mine alone. During one of my excursions, I met a kindly, older lady. Over time I became like a grandson to her, and she became special to me.

When we moved away, I missed seeing her every day, and I especially longed for a piece of her delicious coconut cake. It was the most wonderful concoction that I had ever tasted. Each layer was as light as a cloud, with a soft and silky texture. The icing was a delicate meringue carefully whipped into stiff peaks. The top was dusted with a coating of fresh coconut, grated by hand.

Often I'd run up the flight of stairs that separated our apartments whenever I caught just one whiff. Sometimes I would think that Aunt Elsie baked a cake just to get me to come over to her apartment.

"What would you like for Christmas?" she asked me on the telephone a couple of days before Christmas.

It didn't take me long to decide. "A whole coconut cake, just for me."

I guess she was surprised, or maybe just flattered. But on Christmas Day, she arrived on my doorstep with a silver cake holder in hand. I couldn't have been happier to see her. I enjoyed that cake like none before. But that was just the beginning.

As I grew up, each Christmas came with a fluffy coconut cake. Ten years passed, 20 years passed. Each time Christmas came, Aunt Elsie baked one of her prize-winning creations. Cooking became difficult for her after arthritis set in. One time she was in the hospital when Christmas rolled around, but I still received my coconut cake. She telephoned her husband, and he baked it while she gave him directions from her bed.

Soon the cake became more than a gift. It developed into a tradition of love. I went to college 600 miles away; I received a coconut cake, wrapped in foil, for my birthday via first-class mail. Four years later, I graduated; another cake. I got married five years after that; a hand-delivered cake. Became a father for the first time; cake the next evening.

For many years, I have gotten a coconut cake on special occasions. But more important, I have grown to love someone who started out as just a neighbor. Because of curiosity, and great taste buds, Aunt Elsie is in my life. She's the (coconut) icing on the cake.

BY HARRISON KELLY

Our Growing Family

❦   ❦   ❦

W HEN I AGREED to be the godmother to my sister's two children, I thought it was an honor. I also thought that I would never actually have to become their legal guardian, as most godmothers probably think. But tragically, an auto accident was to take the lives of my sister, Angela, and her husband, Robert. As my entire family tried to cope with the despair, I grieved especially hard for two little girls who no longer had a mother or father.

Jerilynn was only three, and Adrianne was just shy of five, but both were acutely aware that their mommy and daddy were gone. As the days passed, it was obvious that their depression was deepening. I had always been so close to the girls, and now I realized that I was to become their legal guardian, just as I had promised Angela when I agreed to be Godmother.

It had never occurred to me that I would one day take these two children into my own family of four. My husband, Jason, was fully supportive and anxious to welcome the girls into our fold. I wasn't so sure about my two kids, Jason Jr., age five, and Connie, who was almost seven. I knew JJ and Connie loved their cousins and enjoyed spending time with them, but living with them day to day was a completely different story. Would my children be able to accept two new "intruders" into their familial domain? And would they be able to do it only a month before Christmas, a holiday they enjoyed so much because of all the attention Jason and I lavished upon them?

The day that I brought the girls home for the first time as official new members of our family was a day I will never forget. They were silent and almost robotic, following me around as if afraid to be alone. Not once did they say a word, even to my children, with whom they'd always played happily. I had set them up in the spare bedroom so that they could be together, knowing how important it was that they have each other to lean on. It was in that room that they would spend most of the next two weeks, hiding from the world, desperately trying to process what was happening to them.

There were bouts of crying and nightmares and even bursts of rage and anger, and I took each in stride, exercising patience as I gently tried to reach out to these two little birds with broken wings. My kids had not been much help, whining about them and asking when they would go home. I firmly explained that Jeri and Addie were here to stay, that they were now part of our family. The idea was not a popular one, and after a while Jason and I began to wonder if we had taken on more than we could handle.

But after about two weeks, something began to shift. More and more often the two girls would venture downstairs to the kitchen to just sit and watch me cook or clean. They even began to show interest in the cartoons JJ loved to watch, and I noticed smiles on their rosebud lips when Connie asked them to help us make Christmas cookies. They didn't actually help, but they did sit with us and shyly ate our offerings of frosting or broken cookies.

The day Jason brought home the Christmas tree was a breakthrough of sorts. My family made a huge fuss about decorating the tree each year. It took only an hour before Jeri and Addie came downstairs to see what was going on. I noticed that they had been crying, and my first reaction was dread. Had we

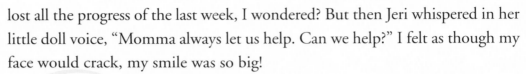

lost all the progress of the last week, I wondered? But then Jeri whispered in her little doll voice, "Momma always let us help. Can we help?" I felt as though my face would crack, my smile was so big!

The week before Christmas, Jason did his usual surprise. He had his roly-poly friend play Santa, and when he showed up at the house in full Santa garb, my kids squealed with delight. JJ and Connie took turns sitting on Santa's knee and reading their lists of desired goodies. I could see Jeri and Addie peeking out of their room, watching, but they closed the door and never opened it again.

After Santa left, I went up to see the girls. They were lying on their beds, tears in their eyes. Jeri was holding her favorite teddy bear tightly. Addie had her arms wrapped around herself as if holding on for dear life. I sat quietly for a moment. Then I asked them why they didn't want to see Santa. After a long silence, Addie mumbled that they always got to see Santa at the local department store. "Daddy took us every year. Santa never came to our house." I realized that even though it wasn't important to me, ritual was very important to two little girls who had lost their parents. I understood then that we had been so busy trying to incorporate them into our idea of what a family was that we had ignored their own ideas.

For the next two hours, I got the girls to tell me stories about their own family's Christmas traditions. I made mental notes on everything, from visiting Santa at the store, to making a cake shaped like a Christmas tree to leave for Santa on Christmas Eve, to something my own family had rarely done: going to church on Christmas Day.

The next night, Jason rounded up the two girls for a special trip to see Santa. My own kids would stay home, as I had explained to them the importance of Jason bonding with the girls. Surprisingly, my kids were totally agreeable, and they even got excited at the thought of doing special things to make the girls feel more at home. It was nice to see JJ and Connie adapting to the idea of an extended family, and we all had a blast that night making a Christmas tree cake to leave for Santa—to Jeri's and Addie's exact specifications, of course.

On Christmas Eve, we all sang carols and ate cookies and told stories about past Christmases. I sensed that the girls needed to talk about their mom and dad, and so we spent some time remembering Angela and Robert, and how special and wonderful they were. As I tucked the girls in for bed, I spent a few moments talking with them about how their parents were always with them in their hearts, and that although I could never replace their mom, I hoped that one day the girls would think of me as a "second mom." "We want to be your family, if that's OK with you," I said softly. By their smiles, I could see it was an idea they were warming up to.

Christmas morning came quickly, and Jason and I exchanged a quick kiss as we headed downstairs to see all four kids crawling like bugs under the tree, piling up gifts and giggling like pixies. We had made sure to buy each child the same amount of

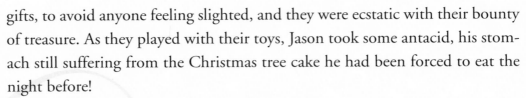

gifts, to avoid anyone feeling slighted, and they were ecstatic with their bounty of treasure. As they played with their toys, Jason took some antacid, his stomach still suffering from the Christmas tree cake he had been forced to eat the night before!

Then we all got dressed in our finest clothes and headed to church. My kids protested at first, wanting to stay and keep playing, but once we got to the service they settled down, even enjoying the celebration of sermons and carols. I hadn't remembered church being so uplifting, and when I saw the look on Jeri's and Addie's faces, I realized that this was one family ritual we would keep forever.

We spent the rest of Christmas Day with visiting relatives, playing with toys, snacking on cookies, and trying to enjoy the day—as much as we could without Angela and Robert. At one point, I was in the kitchen preparing the turkey dinner when little Jeri came running in and just grabbed my leg and hugged me. That's all she did; she didn't even say anything. Just hugged my leg and went running off to join the party in the next room.

When I peeked into the family room, I saw the kids playing and laughing together on the floor while the older relatives talked. The fire was roaring in the fireplace, and carols played softly on the stereo. A feeling of warmth came over me. I whispered a prayer of thanks, and I cried.

BY DAUPHINE JONES

A Present Without Ribbons

❧   ❧   ❧

"WHAT DO YOU MEAN, you have to work Christmas Day?" Ginny stared at her new husband in disbelief. "My family expects us for Christmas dinner!"

"Honey, I'd love to have the day off, but the fire station stays open—even on holidays."

"Well, let some older firefighter take your turn. We've only been married four months. Maybe there's a guy who wouldn't mind working." Ginny knew she was being stubborn, but she couldn't help herself.

"Come on, Ginny. Nobody wants to work on Christmas. But firefighters are like doctors or police officers. People count on us to be available every day of the year. How about if you go on to your parents' for the family party, and in the evening we'll have dinner together and open our presents? It'll be just the two of us in front of a warm fire."

Ginny was truly disappointed. For weeks she'd been imagining how it would feel to attend her family's holiday party as a full-fledged "grown-up," accompanied by her tall, handsome husband. Now her older sisters would include her in their conversations about recipes, mortgages, and husbands who drop their dirty socks on the floor.

On Christmas Day, Ginny found herself answering questions about why Matt wasn't at the party. As she watched her family unwrap presents, chattering excitedly under the beautifully decorated tree, it seemed as if she was the only person in the room who wasn't having a terrific time. She was relieved when it was time to leave.

But things at home weren't what she had imagined. Matt was too tired to enjoy their holiday meal together.

"You aren't eating very much," Ginny complained. She had made Matt's favorite meal—glazed ham with scalloped potatoes and a lemon meringue pie for dessert.

"Sorry, honey, but I'm exhausted. We had an early-morning fire that took most of the day to put out." There were dark circles under his eyes, and Ginny could see traces of grime near his hairline.

"Maybe you should just rest on the sofa for a while. I'll put the food away and load the dishwasher. Then we can open our presents."

Matt stretched out gratefully. Ginny covered him with an afghan and turned on the TV to keep him company while she cleared away the dinner dishes. But when she returned to the living room a few minutes later, he was fast asleep, snoring gently in front of the television. Their presents lay unopened under the tree.

"This is the worst Christmas I've ever had!" Ginny muttered angrily. "I won't get to celebrate with Matt at all!" Feeling sorry for herself, she slumped into a chair and turned up the volume on the evening news.

Suddenly, the screen came alive with a roaring fire. As Ginny leaned forward, she saw a firefighter scaling a ladder against the side of a flame-riddled apartment building.

The newscaster intoned, "Unfortunately, not everyone had a merry Christmas today. At six-thirty this morning, the families in this apartment building lost their presents, their Christmas trees, and their homes. Thanks to the fire department's quick response, however, no lives were lost."

The camera cut to a soot-covered firefighter picking his way carefully down a ladder. Clinging to his neck was a frightened toddler. Ginny knew who the firefighter was even before she saw a close-up of his face. It was Matt.

So she thought *she'd* had a miserable Christmas! What about the fire victims? What about Matt, who had given up his holiday and risked his own life in order to save others? Ginny's cheeks burned when she thought about how self-centered she'd been. True, they hadn't opened their presents yet, but Matt had already given Ginny a wonderful gift: the love of a man who was both courageous and unselfish.

She turned off the lamps so that only the tiny bulbs on their Christmas tree illuminated the room with a soft, cheery glow. *I know how to make things right,* she thought. Tomorrow Matt would wake up to a feast of bacon, eggs, sweet rolls, and freshly brewed coffee. More important: He'd wake up to a happy wife who would tell him she was proud to be married to a hero.

By ANN RUSSELL

A Christmas Present to Brag About

❦ ❦ ❦

"**W**HAT'LL IT BE FOR YOU folks?" the rolling-store man asked as Mama, Dad, and I stepped up to the back of the huge truck that had been converted into a mobile general store. Two battery-powered light bulbs dangling from the ceiling lit up the shelves, where small dolls, toy cars, cap pistols, marbles, harmonicas, pocket knives, candy, apples, oranges, and other Christmas items were stacked in bins along with groceries and other merchandise.

The rolling store was well stocked on the last run before Christmas, and the sight of all those holiday goodies reminded me that I might not—probably would not—get the special present I wanted. And later, when the boys at school would ask what I got for Christmas, I'd have to hear them laugh when I'd mumble, "Oh, this and that." I had dreamed of being able to tell them about a two-key harmonica, a toy dump truck, an air rifle, or even a cheap guitar. I wanted something an 11-year-old boy could brag about to generate envy in his peers.

The last rolling-store run before Christmas was almost as exciting as Christmas Eve for the children in our Appalachian mountain community. That was when the two-ton truck with a huge flat-top box would make its rounds, loaded with as much "Christmas" as it could hold. And children, spying from windows and porches, would speculate wistfully on the contents of paper sacks and cardboard boxes carried to the house.

Even in 1938, though, there were some of us who could not expect much from the rolling store. But we all hoped anyway. We had hoped that year, but I, the oldest of five children, with some understanding of the family finances, didn't see much reason to hope as Christmas approached. It had been a bad year, and all I could expect for Christmas was maybe a bag of marbles and some candy and oranges—certainly nothing to brag about.

Dad had come down with the flu in January, and for two months there were no biscuits in my school lunch bucket, only corn bread, which I was embarrassed to eat in front of the boys whose parents could afford flour, some of the same boys who would ask what I got for Christmas. In late March, a boiling pot overturned on the hearth, scalding the feet of my two-year-old sister, and my younger brother tasted some lye that had been left in a dish. Any extra money had to go to their care.

In May, however, our future seemed brighter when Dad got a job on the new state highway project. The three dollars a day he'd earn would put biscuits on the breakfast table and maybe buy us some new shoes to wear on Sunday. By June, Mama began to talk of some purchases she would like to make—linoleum for the kitchen floor, some cloth for new curtains, maybe even a radio someday so it wouldn't be so lonesome in the house when the children went away to school. That was when I began to dream of harmonicas, guitars, air rifles, and toy trucks.

But then in June, our fortunes changed again. The driver of the panel-body Dodge that took men to work on the highway project appeared at our door one day. He told us Dad had been caught in the path of a sliding rock and had been taken 30 miles to a hospital with a broken leg. Mama hired a neighbor to take her to visit Dad and later to bring him home. In August, he broke the leg again when he jumped from a runaway buggy going down a steep hill. Then in November, he found a temporary job cutting logs, but he owed so much by then—for food, Mama's trips to the hospital, and medicine—that it was not likely there would be any money for Christmas.

But I still listened for the rolling-store horn when it topped the ridge that morning. I traced its progress as its horn signaled the stops along the main road, hoping against hope that I would somehow get a present I wouldn't be ashamed to talk about.

When Mama put the supper on the back of the stove, I realized that she, too, was expecting the rolling store. Around 7:00, she and Dad left my brother and sisters with Grandma and took me with them to the nearby gravel road, where the rolling store made one of its scheduled stops. Seeing us waiting there, the rolling-store man gave a long blast on the horn. "Folks sure buyin' stuff this year fer Christmas," he said. "Looks like a good Christmas for a lot of folks." Again I thought of the present I might not get.

Then Mama began to buy. Oranges. Apples. Candy. Two bags of marbles. Two packs of firecrackers. Three little cheap dolls. Two pairs of gloves. But no harmonica, air rifle, toy truck, or guitar. She also bought some self-rising flour, sugar, chocolate, raisins, bananas, and bologna. As the rolling-store man put the purchases into paper sacks, I wondered if Dad would ask for credit. But to my surprise, he handed the man a $10 bill. "Been savin' this a long time," he said proudly.

But still no present to brag about, I thought. *At least not one from the rolling store.* And where would another present come from now? Soon Christmas would be over, and I would have to answer "this and that" when the boys at school asked about my present.

Christmas morning came cold and frosty, with a sunrise that promised an afternoon warm enough for playing outside—if one had something like a truck or air rifle to play with. Mama woke the girls, who screamed with joy when they pulled the tiny dolls from their stockings. My brother reached into his stocking and brought out gloves, firecrackers, and marbles. "My own marbles!" he yelled. "Big taw, too. Now I can get in the good games at school." While Mama and Dad looked at me, I slowly emptied my stocking and—just as I expected—found gloves, marbles, and fire-crackers. I imagined smirks on the faces of the bragging boys when they would tell me about their presents.

Now the hoping and waiting was over, and Christmas would be a dull day—dinner with Grandpa and Grandma, playing marbles with my brother, and going with Dad to the field to shoot the firecrackers. Meantime, the other boys would be playing with trucks or wagons, trying out their harmonicas, or shooting at old cans with air rifles.

Later, as we gathered at the table for dinner, I felt a nagging in my heart. I looked around at my loving parents, doting grandparents, and smiling siblings, and it occurred to me that maybe, just maybe, I did have something to brag about. I thought about some of those boys who were sure to flaunt their gifts, and I realized that what I had was probably more important. There were the two brothers who were being raised by an indulgent, widowed mother. They might get air rifles, but they would not have a father or grandpa to teach them how to shoot. One boy was from a troubled home often filled with screaming, fighting, and cursing. I knew he wouldn't have a laughing, caring family joining him at his dinner table.

Another boy had a drunken, abusive father who would certainly make Christmas a miserable day for his son, who might have to take refuge in the barn with his present. I knew these boys would all brag to me about their wonderful presents, but I kind of felt sorry for them. I realized they were longing for something they were never going to have, and no amount of harmonicas or toy trucks or guitars could ever make them truly happy.

As we bowed our heads to say grace, I smiled, knowing I was part of a family held together by love, hard work, and hope for better things to come. And that was definitely something to brag about.

BY ERNEST SHUBIRD

If there is no joyous way to give a
festive gift, give love away.
UNKNOWN

From Christmas to Christmas

🌿　　🌿　　🌿

IT WAS EARLY DECEMBER, and I had planned a wonderful holiday for my 13-year-old twins. I wrapped presents, ordered the turkey, and decorated every room of our home. It was difficult without my husband, but the girls always looked forward to Christmas, and it felt good to celebrate again. I was grateful that they were adjusting after the death of their dad three years ago.

Snow had just started to fall when I climbed into my new SUV and began the trip to my office. The picturesque drive to my job at the feed mill gave me time to pray and to appreciate God's handiwork.

At the office, I dropped my purse on my desk and made myself tea. I sorted through the mail, turned off the answering machine, and turned on the gas fireplace. Walter, who owned the feed mill, pulled in, and his son was right behind him.

After a quick exchange of hellos, we settled into our routine. In the late afternoon, Walter motioned me into his office. When he asked me to close the door, I hesitated. But his face didn't change, so I shut the door and sat.

"I need to make some changes," he started, then cleared his throat. "To make this simple, I'm letting you go." He stared at me.

I stared back. "I don't understand."

"We're selling the mill, and in the meantime I need to cut back. Junior can handle the accounts, and my wife can type my letters at home."

"But Walter, it's Christmas. Who's going to buy the feed mill this time of year? What will I tell my girls? I love this job." Words just tumbled out. I knew I wasn't making sense, but I was in shock.

Walter did little to salve my wounded spirit. He asked me to work until the end of the year and said he'd give me a letter of recommendation. A letter. To show to whom? There weren't any jobs out here. I left his office in a daze.

On the ride home, a thousand things went through my mind. How would I tell the twins? Should I return all their presents before the bills appeared on my credit cards? Should I cancel the turkey and ask my mom to have Christmas? But by the time I pulled into my driveway, I knew that I shouldn't tell them just yet. It would only frighten them and ruin their holiday excitement.

To make sure the girls wouldn't find out, I didn't share the news with the rest of my family or my church. I prayed fervently for God to make a way. Some nights I lay awake; some nights I even cried.

I started to recall all the verses I'd ever read about how God took care of his children, and suddenly peace came. I realized that the God who had gotten us through the unexpected death of my husband could get us through this. By comparison, losing my job seemed trivial. The God who had been faithful in the one would be faithful in the other. I thanked him for my sense of peace and went on preparing for the holidays.

And they were grand. On Christmas morning, the twins acted just like teenagers. Every pair of jeans, strand of beads, and pair of socks were oohed and aahed over as if they'd never seen anything like them before. Dinner was marvelous. Their cousins, aunts, uncles, and grandparents did their best to fill any gaps the twins might have felt on this third Christmas without their dad.

Late that evening, the three of us went over the day's events, relishing the surprises and rituals of a large, happy family. After the twins went to bed, I sat alone and studied the flames. I was feeling undeniably strong.

On New Year's Day, I told the girls. They sat silently, taking in the enormity of the situation. They volunteered their savings, their future babysitting money, and to take after-school jobs—all the things I would have expected from them. But I explained my sense of assurance from God, and they nodded appreciatively. We made a prayer pact. We would pray together before they left for school, and then we'd pray at noon, each wherever we were.

Finishing this story with a happily-ever-after ending would be easy, but it would be untrue. Unemployment checks ended all too soon, and we had a few scary moments regarding the mortgage. I gave up my new car, along with its payments, for an older, smaller model. The twins started carrying lunch rather than buying it, and both canceled plans for summer camp. In the fall we lowered the thermostat a degree or two, gave up our Saturday night pizza, and decided on homemade Christmas presents.

According to the Thanksgiving Day paper, the feed mill had sold. I had to admit, almost a year later, I still missed my job. But I didn't let it stop me from dragging boxes of ornaments out of the attic so that we could start putting up our decorations.

On Monday morning, the new owners of the feed mill called and offered me my old job. It was a wonderful Christmas present, and I thanked God for it. More than that, I thanked him for teaching all three of us that we really could rely on him when things got tough.

BY VALORIE NANCE

A Perfect Christmas

❦   ❦   ❦

THROUGHOUT MY LIFE, my mother always tried to make Christmas as warm and joyful as possible. It wasn't always easy for her, and, growing up, we kids didn't always appreciate her efforts. Mom got very sick a month before Christmas 1989 and was admitted to the hospital. When I went to visit her, she didn't seem too concerned about her health; she was more upset about not getting her cooking and shopping done. As usual, Mom's primary concern was for her family. She always wanted the holidays to be perfect for us.

Mom was released two weeks before Christmas, and she immediately dove back into her holiday to-do list. Besides cleaning, cooking, writing out cards, and shopping, Mom stayed up late every night painting and sewing gifts for various relatives. Exhausted, she would sometimes burst into tears, afraid she wouldn't get everything done in time and Christmas would be ruined.

My parents had divorced when I was nine years old. Even though my mom had no job or other source of income at the time, she fought for—and won—the custody of her four children. She knew it would be a struggle, but Mom believed the most important thing was to hold her family together as much as possible. She was forced to rely on welfare for a while, and she and my father were constantly battling. Eventually she got a good job, but even during the toughest times, she always kept a roof over our heads and plenty of laughter in our hearts.

As I entered my teenage years, I didn't notice how hard Mom worked for us or the sacrifices she made on our behalf. All I cared about were the things I felt I was missing out on. I resented our financial situation, and I hated not having my dad around. Eventually I began to take it out on my mom. We fought all the time, and I'm sure I said some mean, regretful things. I realize now that this was another burden added to my mom's already overwhelming list. But she never took her anger or frustration out on us. Even when she worked so hard for so little appreciation, my mother continued to make her children the main priority in her life.

It wasn't until that Christmas in 1989 that I finally realized once and for all what a blessing our mother has been. On Christmas Eve, my family and I went to my cousin's house for dinner. Even as an adult, I still felt a twinge of jealousy because they all had their parents with them. They hadn't had to deal with custody battles and constant fighting and never-ending financial sacrifices. As wonderful as it was to spend time with my extended family, a part of my heart still ached for the childhood I felt I'd missed out on.

After dinner, we went back to Mom's house; she had stayed behind to finish the last of her holiday tasks. Even though she was still recovering from her recent illness, she didn't let that slow her down. When I opened the front door, I nearly gasped. Dozens of lit candles made the whole house glow, and Christmas music was playing softly. The lush, fragrant tree, covered in handmade ornaments, twinkled brightly, and carefully wrapped gifts surrounded its base. I couldn't have created a more perfect holiday scene in my deepest childhood dreams. Mom smiled and laughed as she welcomed us in, taking our coats and offering steaming cups of hot cider.

Then she started handing out her specially made presents, much to the delight of everyone in the room. It was at that moment I realized how much I had taken her for granted all those years. As I looked around, I smiled, even as tears welled up in my eyes. There wasn't a single thing missing in my house: There were stacks of presents, freshly baked cookies, easy laughter, and heart-felt sharing. But most important, there was a feeling of warmth and safety, of love and family and home.

My mom had done all of this, with her own hands, by herself, because she wanted to. She knew the true meaning of Christmas, and somehow, without a single word, she finally taught it to me: It's not the presents or the cookies that really matter—it's who you share them with.

BY MICHELLE KLEIBER

The earth has grown old with its burden of care
But at Christmas it always is young,
The heart of the jewel burns lustrous and fair
And its soul full of music breaks the air,
When the song of angels is sung.

PHILLIPS BROOKS

The Christmas Thief

❦ ❦ ❦

"THANK GOD YOU WEREN'T there when it happened." Our mother's hands clutched the telephone receiver. "You might have been injured, or worse."

My brother Thomas and I exchanged worried glances. It was just past 9:00 P.M. on Christmas Eve 1962, and we were waiting for our dad to come home for the Christmas holiday. Company downsizing had eliminated his long-held local job, and, at 52 years old, Dad was forced by financial circumstances to take a position with a firm located two hours away by car. Dad wouldn't consider relocating his family. With the job market so uncertain, he wasn't even sure he'd still have this current job within a year. He felt it was best for the family to stay in our familiar Brooklyn neighborhood.

The commute was hard on Dad, and he and Mom decided that he'd only come home on weekends and major holidays. Friday nights became a time of joy, while Sunday nights were dreaded. Good-byes never got any easier.

"The children will understand," Mom said into the phone. "You just be careful."

Mom hung up and took a deep breath before turning to face us. Before she even said a word, Thomas and I sensed that the news wasn't good.

"That was Dad. His car was stolen, and he's stranded in the town where he works. You both know that without a car Dad needs to take a bus and then three different trains. Since it's already so late, and since some of the depot locations are so desolate, Dad thinks it's best if he waits until tomorrow before attempting the trip."

We understood, but tears sprang to my eyes. I was nine years old, and this was the first year I was considered mature enough to attend midnight mass with my family. Thomas, at 11 years old, was a midnight mass veteran, and his tales of the grand celebration made me even more eager to attend. But without Dad in our pew, I knew my first midnight mass experience would be sadly lacking.

"That's not all." The tensing of Mom's jaw betrayed the feelings she was trying to hide. "You know how much Dad hates having to be away from us all. So this year, in order to feel like he was still very much a part of our lives, he decided to do all the Christmas shopping."

"Dad must have liked that," Thomas pointed out. "Instead of just sitting in his room at the boarding house every night after work, he had something fun to do."

"Dad had everything wrapped, ready to be placed beneath the tree as soon as he got home." Mom's brows drew together in an agonized expression. "He packed them in the trunk of the car this morning so he could leave for home right from work."

Thomas said the words I couldn't. "But the car was stolen, and all the packages were in it."

"Yes," Mom said as she flicked an imaginary speck of dust from her dress, fighting to keep her fragile control. "Even if the stores were still open, there isn't any money to replace what was lost."

A tumble of confused thoughts and feelings assailed me, and I faltered in the silence that engulfed the room. Thomas and I knew Dad had taken a large pay cut, which had meant sacrifices for all of us. Our Christmas tree was much smaller than in other years, and we were having turkey for Christmas dinner instead of the more costly roast beef. Even our Christmas wish list had contained just a few items. Had Dad gotten the miniature race car for Thomas and the golden-haired Barbie for me? How about the warm bathrobe Mom desperately needed?

"I hate the man who robbed our car!" The words burst from my lips. "He took Christmas away from us and I wish . . . I wish the man would just die!"

"Jacquelyn Maria Bernadette Clements! Such a terrible thing for you to say!" Mom glared at me, frowning. "What the man did was wrong, but you must pity him. Lord knows what sort of desperate situation he's in that it drove him to steal, especially on Christmas Eve."

My eyes met Mom's disparagingly, and my lower lip trembled. I wanted to scream at her how our car was gone and we could not afford another, but my brother's hand on my arm silenced me. He was right. What good would it do?

"When you're in church tonight, Jacquelyn, I think you should thank God for what we do have." Mom spoke quietly, but firmly. "Sometimes the most important things in life are those you can't hold in your hand."

I'd lost interest in attending midnight mass, but at 11:30 Mom helped us bundle up for the four-block walk. I had never been out at that hour. The sound of ice crunching underfoot was a counterpoint to the still night and the black sky, which was illuminated by the moon and stars.

Our church interior was all my brother had claimed it would be. The bright moon allowed the arched stained glass windows to flood the house of worship with brilliant, colorful light. Ornate candles and flowers filled the altar, while parishioners who were dressed to portray various biblical characters took their places around the stable replica. Even the choir was brightly attired, ready to sing in celebration of our Lord's birth.

While Father Quinn said the mass, I struggled to find something to be thankful for. We had no money, no car, no Christmas. I couldn't recall the last time Thomas and I went to a Saturday matinee with our friends, and Mom didn't even bake our favorite chocolate chip cookies anymore. Food necessities, such as milk and bread, came first, and there was rarely any money left over for sweets of any kind. Even our yearly summer visit to our grandparents was doubtful with bus fares being what they were.

The sudden cry of the baby portraying the Christ child drew my attention to the stable scene. But my eyes traveled past the infant, lovingly held in the arms of the Mother Mary actress, and came to rest on a figure who had just entered through the side church door. It was Dad!

A joy like I had never known swelled upward, lifting with it all the shadows that darkened my young heart. I poked Thomas and pointed; he did the same to Mom. Our already crowded pew-mates slid over a bit more so Dad could squeeze in with us. Our family clasped hands, and I realized I had found something to be thankful for: Despite all odds, Dad was home for Christmas.

"It was more than a coincidence—it was divine intervention," Dad later explained. "A truck driver in the phone booth next to mine overheard my conversation, and he insisted on helping me get home. He used his radio to contact other drivers along the way, and at rest stops I was passed from one truck to another. Each driver took me as far as he could, the last one dropping me off right in front of the church."

The kindness of strangers on a cold winter's night was another thing for me to be thankful for. The third blessing arrived on Christmas Day, when our car was found abandoned about 100 miles from where it had been stolen. There was minor front-end damage but, surprisingly, the trunk was never opened. All our Christmas gifts were safe.

Only hours before, this fact would have mattered more to me than anything else. However, it provided a mere jump on my happiness scale as I sat playing Monopoly with Dad.

How right Mom had been when she told me, "Sometimes the most important things in life are those you can't hold in your hand." The spirit of Christmas dwells within our hearts, and no one, not even the most skilled thief, can ever take it away.

BY JACKIE CLEMENTS-MARENDA

When Do You Take Down Your Holiday Tree?

❦ ❦ ❦

As a youngster, I used to rush to clear the dishes from our Thanksgiving table, hoping I could hurry Christmas all the faster. The end of Thanksgiving signaled that Christmas was near, and the magic of that season made my whole year worthwhile. It still does.

But all too soon Christmas is over. The tree is carried to the curb, the decorations are hauled to the attic, and holiday dishes are packed away for another year. The pure-white snow that made Christmas postcard-perfect quickly becomes muddy brown slush, seeping into boots and splashing the hems of our coats.

My mood used to darken, too. I'd notice a dried-up evergreen wreath still hanging from a front door or Christmas lights drooping from someone's gutters and I'd turn mean. I mentally berated them for tarnishing Christmas on their front lawns. What were they? Lazy?

Then, this spring, long after the daffodils had appeared in my backyard, I overheard a conversation at the deli counter in the supermarket. Two elderly gentlemen were discussing the recent deaths of their wives.

"It's peculiar," one said, "but I still have my Christmas wreath hanging on my front door. I just can't seem to take it down. My wife loved that wreath, the smell, the color of the ribbon, the pinecones. It was the last Christmas wreath she ever picked out." He shook his head.

"I know," the other man responded. "My wife died in January, and I left our Christmas decorations out until Easter. Just couldn't bear to put them away, knowing she would never see them again."

I learned something that day in the supermarket, and I've never looked at "delinquent" Christmas decorations in the same way. Now when I see a home bedraggled in holiday splendor in the middle of March, I wonder if the ornaments offer some kind of comfort or solace—some link to a happier past. Then I murmur a heartfelt prayer with the sincere intention that springtime will enter their home again.

BY BARBARA DAVEY

There's more, much more to Christmas
Than candlelight and cheer;
It's the spirit of sweet friendship
That brightens all the year;
It's thoughtfulness and kindness,
It's hope reborn again,
For peace, for understanding
And for good will to men!

ANONYMOUS

Away for the Holidays

CHRISTMAS . . . is not an eternal event at all, but a
piece of one's home that one carries in one's heart.

FREYA STARK (1893–1993)
"THE WISE MEN"

Christmas Abroad

❧ ❧ ❧

*S*UE HAD NEVER FELT so alone in all her life. Surrounded by people in a busy, noisy, hectic urban setting, she felt cut off from everyone. She heard the steady buzz of voices as crowds pressed around her, but not a single word could she understand. In another country, where she scarcely spoke a word of the language, Sue felt strange and lost.

Worst of all, it was almost Christmas. Back home the stores were undoubtedly jammed full of merchandise, decorated with green and red ornaments, with familiar music filling the air. Corner Santas would be jingling their bells amid lightly falling snow. Crowds of shoppers would be rushing to get their gift buying done, while children with excited voices and eager eyes would wait in line to sit on Santa's lap.

Sue had been so wrapped up in preparing for her move to Belgium that she'd hardly thought about what it would be like being so far from home. Adjusting to another country, even one fairly similar to her own, hadn't seemed difficult when she'd first thought about it.

There'd be changes, of course. She knew that. She'd begun studying the language. But her skills were so lacking that she could hardly follow even the most basic comments. And living here now, she realized that life moved at a fast pace, with people chatting rapidly in their own language the way she'd spoken in English back home. Everything was harder here than she'd expected,

more complicated and confusing, more demanding. Everything took longer because she wasn't familiar with customs and patterns.

So far, she had been lost so often that it seemed the norm. She carried a map of the city with her everywhere, but she usually couldn't follow directions when someone seemed willing to help. She carried a basic phrase book along with her, too. But somehow the phrases she needed never seemed to be in the book—or else her pronunciation was so terrible that no one understood her.

And now here it was, Christmas season rapidly approaching, and Sue felt more homesick than she could ever have imagined. She had made no friends. Nothing felt right here in this strange land. Unable to express herself much of the time, she had begun feeling incredibly stupid and inept.

It was time to shop for gifts. Time to hang decorations and trim a tree. Time to mail cards and write cheery notes in them. Determined to get ready for the season, Sue ventured into the city, pushing aside her anxieties. She couldn't help worrying. What if she got lost again? What if she missed the last bus for home because she misread the schedule—she'd already almost done that once. What if she wandered into a bad neighborhood or had her purse stolen or stumbled into some crisis and couldn't ask for help?

But she was determined. No matter how uneasy she felt, she would set off in this strange land to find some way to prepare for the holidays. She searched store aisles until she found what looked like Christmas gift wrap, though the texture was different and the colors not quite what she'd expected. She found greeting cards, too, though she wasn't entirely certain what the words meant. She found gifts to send to her family back home, and she managed to count out the cash to pay for them. And in the market, she found what she hoped

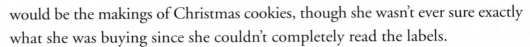

would be the makings of Christmas cookies, though she wasn't ever sure exactly what she was buying since she couldn't completely read the labels.

Yet, to Sue's surprise, everywhere she went she found kindness. As she fumbled with words and money, strangers patiently offered help. When she tried to buy stamps at the post office for her cards, a kind-faced stranger smiled and corrected her word choice (Sue had asked for tombstones by mistake). A lady at the bus stop, as heavily laden with packages as Sue, studied the map Sue held out and helped her find the right bus.

When a great crowd of people crammed into what they thought to be the last bus, Sue joined the laughter and waved as an empty bus passed them from behind. At her own apartment, a neighbor held the tiny elevator door open for her. She helped her squeeze in her tubes of gift wrap, which were almost too long to fit inside.

The days flew by as Sue prepared for the holidays. Nothing was the same as it would have been at home, but some things were better in their own way. Visiting neighbors brought boxes of candy or cut flowers (it wasn't polite to drop by without some small gift), and she happily greeted them with the few words she'd practiced in their language. She began to make friends, one of whom introduced her to the paper-wrapped snack of waffles, which one could carry in one hand while shopping.

Sue's "Christmas tree" was simply a potted plant with paper ornaments hung on it, but it brought smiles and nods of appreciation from her neighbors. Nearby shop owners had become familiar to her. They greeted her with smiles and words spoken slowly so that she could understand, and they even knew her regular purchases.

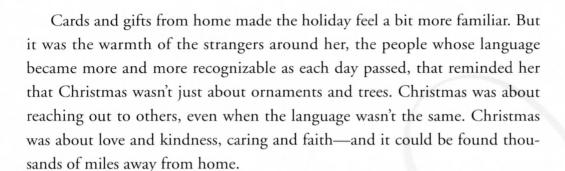

Cards and gifts from home made the holiday feel a bit more familiar. But it was the warmth of the strangers around her, the people whose language became more and more recognizable as each day passed, that reminded her that Christmas wasn't just about ornaments and trees. Christmas was about reaching out to others, even when the language wasn't the same. Christmas was about love and kindness, caring and faith—and it could be found thousands of miles away from home.

BY PATRICIA MURPHY

AWAY IN A MANGER

Away in a manger, no crib for a bed,
The little Lord Jesus laid down his sweet head.
The stars in the sky looked down where he lay,
The little Lord Jesus asleep in the hay.

The cattle are lowing, the baby awakes,
But little Lord Jesus no crying he makes.
I love Thee, Lord Jesus, look down from the sky
And stay by my cradle til morning is nigh.

Be near me, Lord Jesus, I ask Thee to stay
Close by me forever, and love me, I pray.
Bless all the dear children in thy tender care,
And take us to heaven, to live with Thee there.

MARTIN LUTHER (1483–1546)

Christmas Without Snow?

❧   ❧   ❧

"**W**HY DO WE HAVE to go anywhere for Christmas?" Louise asked her mother, Maggie, in her snippy little eight-year-old voice. "I like to be here. Santa is here; he knows where I am, and I don't want to leave. Why do we have to go? Besides, how can we have Christmas without snow? It doesn't snow there. I don't want to go to the beach on Christmas. That's dumb."

"What is dumb, Louise, is the way you are continuing to harass your whole family about this trip. It is not about you. It is about Aunt Sandra and her new baby."

"Well, why should I care about her new baby? I don't even know her. Besides, what does a stupid baby know about Santa Claus or Christmas? And she will never know what snow is like, so who cares about her?"

"I will try to pretend you don't know what you're whining about. But you sound really selfish right now. And what do you care about Santa? You told me last month that Santa is a story that everyone makes up." Louise let out a huge sigh, pursed her lips, and stormed to her bedroom, slamming the door behind her.

Her father started after her, but his wife gently placed her hand on his arm and stopped him. "Ted, don't upset yourself. She is too little to understand anything but her own little world. Your sister would be disappointed if we didn't make this trip. Everything is in place, and I refuse to upset myself because our daughter is acting like a spoiled child. Maybe every kid gets like this once in a while, huh? Even our precious little angel." Maggie smiled, and that seemed to take the edge off the little scene that just played out.

The only good news for Louise was that she could leave school early because the long drive to South Carolina would take a few days. Louise's teacher gave her a little assignment. She was to keep a journal of what she saw and the things she did while she was away. "One more icky thing to do," she muttered to herself.

"No snow," Louise told her friend, Mary Ellen. "Can you imagine that? I'll be spending Christmas with a screaming baby, and there won't be any snow. What am I supposed to do all day? Am I supposed to pick that moss junk from the trees and make snowballs out of it?"

"Maybe you can stay with me until your parents get back," Mary Ellen offered. Both second graders already knew the answer.

Three days before Christmas, Louise's parents packed the van, picked up Louise's grandparents, and headed south. They drove through the snows of New York and Pennsylvania, then through Maryland and Virginia. Louise's father remarked that he was surprised to see snow in Richmond, and Louise quipped, "Well, why don't we just turn around here and head home? Then we could see snow all week long." Her parents simply ignored her.

The few flurries over Richmond turned into blue skies in North Carolina. South Carolina was warm, sunny, and decorated for Christmas. It did look a bit odd to have Christmas signs and decorations in temperatures of 65 degrees. Even odder was the sight of a decorated Christmas tree in a house with open doors and windows.

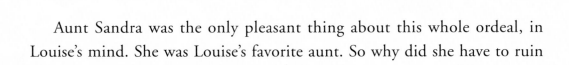

Aunt Sandra was the only pleasant thing about this whole ordeal, in Louise's mind. She was Louise's favorite aunt. So why did she have to ruin everything by having a child?

On Christmas Day, they all went to church; even the baby went. They walked on the sandy streets, and somehow Louise ended up pushing the baby's carriage.

On Christmas night they decided to take a drive and look at the decorations in the neighborhood. They piled into the car, with the baby ending up on Louise's lap. The baby stared at her cousin, and Louise worked very hard at trying to ignore her without letting her fall on the floor.

By the day after Christmas, Louise's baby cousin was fussing for Louise to hold her. Louise grudgingly obliged the little intruder. Then, Louise discovered that something fascinating was beginning to happen. This child was smiling at her and touching her face and falling asleep in her arms. And it felt good. And this baby smelled good. She smelled like . . . well, she smelled like a baby.

The next day, Louise asked her Aunt Sandra if she could take the baby for a walk in the stroller. "After all, it is a beautiful day and there's no snow, so we can go down to the beach. The wheels won't get stuck in slush like they would in New York." Sandra smiled at her niece, gave her a hug, and put a sweater on both girls. Louise and Maggie took the baby for a stroll, and when they returned, Louise sat with her and played with her and fed her and rocked her to sleep.

Before Louise knew it, it was time to turn around and head north again. Christmas was over and the disastrous trip to South Carolina was nearing its end. She thought about it and wondered how she would be able to live in New

York without this sweet little bundle of baby who adored her. Aunt Sandra assured her that when school was finished in June, she could come to South Carolina for a visit.

Louise spent most of the car trip home writing about things she saw and what she did. When she returned to New York, Mary Ellen came to visit Louise. She bounded in the door barely a minute after the car pulled into the garage.

"Well, how did you manage Christmas without any snow?"

Louise looked at her friend with a puzzled look on her face and said, "Honestly, Mary Ellen! There really are more important things about Christmas than whether or not it snows."

BY ELIZABETH TOOLE

So remember while December
Brings the only Christmas Day,
In the year let there be Christmas
In the things you do and say;
Wouldn't life be worth the living
Wouldn't dreams be coming true
If we kept the Christmas spirit
All the whole year through?

AUTHOR UNKNOWN

Happy Holidays From Vietnam

❦   ❦   ❦

CHUCK SAID THAT SOME Christmases are better than others and some are worse. He was right. Pretty profound for a guy sitting around with a bunch of other guys as we prepared to celebrate Christmas in Vietnam. I've been here for about six months, and that statement is the only thing that makes me think beyond the next minute. . . .

Christmas in Vietnam could be any number of celebrations depending on the assignment; I was assigned heavy equipment . . . a member of the Engineers Division. I am in the field with no links to civilization other than the men I was assigned with. . . . Christmas will be what we create.

The Vietcong and their government claimed a cease-fire for this holiday. However, they were the ones who also released the Tet Offensive, which no one was prepared for. So we can only hope and pray that the day, from midnight to midnight, will be quiet and death free. . . . How will my family, especially my mother, ever get through Christmas knowing that I could die today? . . .

I know that there are some things that can make this day better. I am able to look at the men I am sitting with and thank God that they are good men who I can and do trust my life with. I am also lucky because the huge piece of equipment that I care for can also take care of me. . . . The flip side is that I look around at this beautiful country and wonder why I am here. Does God have a plan in all this, and what can his purpose be?

I glance around the area. . . . I see everyone in a happy mood. I know that we can depend on each other and it will help all of us enjoy Christmas. The odd thing is that we don't go anywhere or do anything without our weapons. I don't think that's what the Lord had in mind, but sometimes the master plan has to be altered a little.

Tommy asked us to eat dinner as a group. We wouldn't have to eat canned rations or the sardines my mother regularly sends to replenish salt. Nah, this time we would eat well because the supply drops came on time. . . . Fresh steaks, potatoes, beer, cookies. . . . I might miss turkey, but steak sounds great!

This is probably the first Christmas that I've realized how unimportant presents are. Another hour of peace without an explosion is gift enough. Tommy suggested we tell how we usually spend Christmas. I thought it was an OK idea . . . we all did. Not everyone actually celebrates Christmas, but they were willing to join us Christians for lack of anything better to do.

Tommy tells us that he is from the Midwest. We know that. . . . He grew up on a farm and has a big family. Christmas at his house is a chaotic mix of food, people, and work. . . . The cows need to be milked no matter what day it is. They still produce, even on holidays! Juan's roots are in Puerto Rico. He tells us about the bright colors on the houses and the roar of the ocean and their heroes: golfer Chi Chi Rodriguez, who works with orphans, and Roberto Clemente, the great Pirates outfielder with the rifle arm. . . .

Jack is our golden boy from San Francisco. He dreams of going home for R&R and not coming back. If he did that, he'd have to take off for Canada.... Chuck is from Louisiana. His big dinner is Creole, and he has cousins in 12 shades of skin, from beige to chocolate.

I close my eyes and see that six-foot tree with colored lights, strings of tinsel, and all kinds of decorations that my mother has collected and placed in just the right spot, like she always does. I can smell the turkey and stuffing. Upstate New York is like the Midwest. We are simple, down-to-earth people. I like the Bills... look forward to seeing them play again....

Mike laughs as he tells us that he did not know what a holiday dinner was until he met his wife. His big dinner had been typical Pilgrim grub—a turkey with parsnips and a bowl of soup and bread. Then he discovered stuffing and mashed potatoes and gravy... her family knows how to eat!

I see a camaraderie here. We live in different worlds, but it is all the same world. We worship in different religions, but we have one God.... I know that, so do Tommy and Chuck and Juan and Mike... even Jack. I usually don't say much about God... none of us do. In fact, we don't say much at all... but today we are homesick. I really want to be in my house with my family... we all do. We want peace today, and we want to ask God to keep us safe today, for another day, each day for six more months... because we all want to go home.

I guess we can thank God for this quiet day and for no rain.... I was told the rainy season will be coming... actually, I could use a decent bath.... Rain might not be so bad.... Christmas is like any other day, but I know it gives us a time to stop the war... even if only for a minute or an hour or a day....

By Thomas O'Rourke

Let It Snow

"**W**ASN'T TONIGHT'S SERVICE wonderful, Beth?"

"Hmm? I'm sorry. What did you say, dear?"

Roe glanced at his wife. "I asked what you thought of the Christmas Eve program."

"Nice. It was . . . nice." Beth looked over her shoulder. All three kids slumped against each other in the backseat, sound asleep.

"But?"

Beth didn't answer. She turned to stare out the windshield. A steady stream of traffic slinked like a glowworm, inching its way along the interstate at the foothills of Colorado's Front Range.

"Beth? What's wrong?"

"Wrong? Oh, I'm not sure that anything in particular is wrong, but it's not exactly right, either." She sighed. "Or maybe it's just that everything is . . . so different."

"Well, this isn't Minnesota," Roe chuckled.

"No, it's not, and that's the problem. I guess I'm homesick. Christmas in Minnesota was . . ." Beth's voice trailed off, and her mind followed. Christmas—in Minnesota.

In Minnesota, where stars glittered over a frozen wonderland. How well she knew those winter scenes with steepled churches, fence posts, fields, and barns. All covered with icy snow, wonderful for sledding and old-fashioned sleigh rides and building igloos and forts and massive snow sculptures and . . .

Christmas—at church.

At church, where friends whispered seasonal greetings. Where aunts, uncles, and giggling young cousins crowded into pews. Where grandparents still sang the old carols in Norwegian.

Christmas—at home.

Where getting a tree meant a trip to the woods on the family farm and a lively debate over the merits of each person's chosen favorite. Grandpa's axe always made the first cut, and the kids dragged the tree to the car by its trunk, and sticky sap glued their mittens to the bark.

To her, Christmas *was* Minnesota. Her childhood was gift-wrapped in those warm memories of tradition, and she had planned on more of the same for her own kids. Until this move changed everything.

Instead, here they were, heading back to a new house in a new neighborhood after participating in a *different* Christmas Eve service, with new people in a new church.

"I'm sorry, Roe," Beth said. "Tonight's program really went well. I guess I just missed our traditional sing-along, bell choir, and candlelight vespers."

"Different places do different things, Beth. You'll get used to it." Roe signaled to change lanes.

"I suppose."

"Truthfully, I think your homesickness is nothing that a good snowfall couldn't cure." Roe eased the car toward the exit ramp.

"Well, I must admit, when we moved here in September and I got my first glimpse of those towering Rocky Mountains, I just assumed snowy winters were a given." Beth looked at the dark peaks silhouetted against the clear night sky and shivered. "All this cold weather and not a flake in sight...."

"Only in the upper elevations," Roe said. He pointed to Long's Peak, the favored hiking destination of the locals. "There's the nearest snow—and plenty of it."

"A lot of good that does!"

"It's probably only an hour's drive to the trail head. What do you say we head up there tomorrow with the kids and spend Christmas afternoon in the mountains?"

Beth grimaced. Spending part of Christmas Day driving to find snow didn't fit her mood.

"It's not the same as shoveling sidewalks or building a snowman in the yard or making an arsenal," she said. "Remember the snowball fights we used to have?"

Roe and Beth grinned at each other.

"Yeah," Roe said. "In fact, just today I was telling Ben Johnston across the street how much we'll miss the neighborhood snowball challenges we hosted in Minnesota each Christmas. He got a good chuckle when I told him it was kids against adults—and the adults usually lost."

"That's what I want for Christmas, Roe. I want to look out the window on Christmas morning and see something more than winter-brown grass. I want snow and an old-fashioned snowball fight with friends. Is tradition too much to ask for?"

Slowing, Roe turned down Logan Drive.

"Oh, Beth, I'm sorry this move has been so rough on . . . Well, I'll be!" Roe braked in the middle of the street. "Look!"

Beth gasped. Their lawn—bare and brown only hours before—was covered with several inches of snow. The grass, the walks, the porch, and the bushes all sparkled under the streetlight's glow.

"Snow, kids, snow! Wake up and look at our yard!"

Rubbing sleep from their eyes, all three kids tumbled from the car and raced to the glittery powder. Beth and Roe sat, spellbound.

"I can't believe my eyes," said Beth. "Snow! Snow! But—it's only in *our* yard. How . . . ? And why?"

"Who knows, hon? But you certainly got your Christmas wish."

Roe pointed down the street. "Well, would you look at that!" Ben Johnston's muddied pickup—loaded with snow blowers and shovels, headlights dimmed—slipped around the corner, leaving a fine trail of white.

Roe smiled at his wife. "What do you say we revive an old snowball tradition," he said, "with a brand new neighborhood of friends!"

BY CAROL MCADOO REHME

We shall find peace. We shall hear the angels. We shall see the sky sparkling with diamonds.

ANTON CHEKHOV

Her Christmas Stocking

❦   ❦   ❦

I GOT OFF THE ELEVATOR on the third floor of the retirement home in western Illinois and started down the long hallway to her room. This wasn't how it was supposed to be. Your mom is always supposed to be your mom—just like you have always known her.

Tears came to my eyes, knowing I wasn't going home this year to the familiar rooms and the savory aroma of turkey and dressing, pumpkin pie, and sugar cookies. As I approached Room 327, I saw it—the Christmas stocking hanging on her door. It had such a message for me.

Mom had always been the creative one—the one who normally would have made something for me to hang on *my* door. But now the years have changed my mother. Her fingers can no longer thread the needles. Her eyes can't see the stitches. But the saddest of all: Her mind can no longer focus long enough to complete any project.

So early in November, I gave it my best. I found a piece of old wine-colored velvet. And I remembered a box Mom had given me when she got rid of most of her possessions. In the box were lots of cords of antique lace that had belonged to my father's Aunt Grace. Faded by years, the lace was perfect to cut and glue on the Christmas stocking I had made from the old velvet. The stocking looked as though it had been hung on a door for lots of previous holidays. It seemed to say, "Treasure the past. Hold onto the memories."

The fact that Mom hung the stocking I had made on her door symbolized to me that our roles had been reversed. Now it was my turn to take care of her. Since she had always been there for me, I would now be there for her. I had never imagined this day would be so painful.

Then I saw the nativity scene someone had set up on a small, round table at the end of the hall. The silver figures stood out on the red, flowing tablecloth. I focused on the Christ Child in the lowly manger and then back at the stocking on her door. I knew it was my time to be there for my mother, but was it also time for me to be there for my God? He had always been there for me. He had given that babe in the manger for me. And I had never really accepted the gift.

I couldn't stop the aging process in the mother I knew, but suddenly the words from an old hymn—one of the first I had learned to play on the piano when I was eight years old—came to mind: "Rock of Ages, cleft for me." With that song in my heart, I knocked on Mother's door. She opened it slowly. "Merry Christmas, Mom! I'm home!"

BY ELAINE SLATER REESE

Christmas in Taos

I THINK IT WAS KIT's idea that we all get together in Taos, New Mexico, for Christmas. When I heard the suggestion, I knew right away that it was something we needed to do.

We had just left the memorial service for our sister Margie's husband, Dan, and we were each trying to deal with our own shock and grief. Shock seems an odd word to use when Dan had been fighting cancer for a year and a half. Though we'd all had high hopes for a full recovery for much of that first year, in the last several months it had become increasingly clear that Dan's time was drawing near. So why do I say we were in shock? Maybe we were shocked that it could actually happen to us, shocked that our sister—only 40 years old—could be a widow, shocked that a strong man in the prime of life could succumb, despite the best that modern medicine could offer.

After the service, we stayed in California for a while, trying to help Margie by encouraging her to talk, by distracting her, by simply being there for her. Finally, we all went home: Kit to New Mexico, and my husband, our children, and I back to Iowa. We each had lives, jobs, and school to get on with. Yet it felt jarring to be apart, and though we talked to each other frequently, we worried about our sister and our little niece, Kate, all alone out there in California. Worse yet, the holidays were approaching. Even if we all went back to be with her, we knew the house held too many memories for our sister to deal with

right now. We had all grown up in Maryland, and our parents still lived there, but right now there were too many memories there, also.

That's when Kit had the idea of Christmas in Taos. We could all come to Taos, she proposed, certain that the natural beauty of the Sangre de Cristo Mountains, the unique Southwestern culture, and the rarefied atmosphere at 7,000 feet were sure to lift our spirits.

"On Christmas Eve we can go out to the Pueblo," she told us excitedly. "They'll have bonfires and processionals with chanting and singing. And, if we want, we can go to the Pueblo again on Christmas morning, when they'll do the Deer Dance—something you've really got to see."

And it was something I'd always wanted to see, ever since Kit had moved to New Mexico and opened the door on a world that has existed for over a thousand years but which we, growing up in the East, had only become aware of in the last decade or so. Like many before us, my sisters, our mother, and I found something stirring and exciting in the Native American culture and felt honored that the Pueblo would welcome visitors on such holy days. I agreed with Kit that it would be good for Margie and Kate to be in an unfamiliar place, one that would captivate with its timeless beauty and not haunt them with memories of better days.

"But where will we all stay?" I asked. A good question, too, since Kit lived in a tiny place and accommodations at this time of the year would likely be expensive.

"I might be able to find some house-sits that are either free or cheap," she replied. "I'm sure there are people leaving for the holidays who need someone to take care of their houseplants, puppies, or cats. I'll ask around." Good thing we all like animals, I thought.

Our parents were excited to hear of our tentative plans. Unfortunately, our father's poor health would keep them both at home, but they surprised us by offering to help with travel expenses so the rest of us could go.

"We think it's important for you girls to all be together, and especially to help Margie and Katie through this Christmas," they told us. "And you can bet we'll be there with you in spirit, if not in the flesh."

All that remained was for Kit to find us places to stay. The first house she found was the right size for Margie and Kate—a modern home on a hillside with two cats and a view. As the days wore on, I steeled myself to the likelihood that my husband, daughters, and I would celebrate Christmas crammed into an overpriced hotel room. Then, just in time, Kit called me with the good news: She found us a beautiful adobe in the country with two big dogs. The owners even offered to put up and decorate a big Christmas tree for the kids!

As anyone who's traveled with children at Christmas can attest, it's a big production. No matter where you go, Santa must be able to find you. There must be presents, a tree, and stockings hung or else it's just not Christmas. Fortunately, we took our van. It was a relief to get on the road, especially after a night of packing and repacking an unwieldy assortment of Christmas gifts.

Margie had solved that problem by postponing gift buying until the last minute. It was wise for several reasons, not the least of which was that it must have been less poignant and depressing to shop in a new and exotic place like Taos.

As we drove through the Sangre de Cristo Mountains, climbing from Santa Rosa to Taos, a light snow fell, turning the magnificent landscape into a live Christmas card. Dusk settled in as we arrived in Taos. As we followed the directions to our house, we passed many homes whose graceful silhouettes and flowing patio walls were outlined with traditional luminaria, little paper bags weighted with sand and illuminated with small candles.

Our house was wonderful, with solid adobe walls, exposed viga beams in the ceiling, a brick floor, large windows, lots of plants, two standard poodles (and several strays), and a neighboring pasture with horses. We stood in a field throwing balls for the dogs, breathing deeply the sweet mountain air.

Taos is known for its strong artistic community, and Margie was a fledgling artist herself, having taken up watercolors as a means of expression about midway through Dan's illness. As it happened, Kit's sweetheart, Jon, is an extremely talented and successful artist, best known for his luminous watercolors.

A year earlier, Jon had lost his father to cancer, and he thus felt a kinship to Margie in her loss. Recognizing her interest in art, he invited her to work with him in his studio and shared with her some of his own watercolor techniques. He also took her to visit another famous Taos artist, who gave Margie a rare personal tour of his studio.

Meanwhile, Kit decorated Jon's historic adobe for our sumptuous Christmas Eve feast: walls adorned with beautiful paintings, fire crackling in the

hearth, a blend of Southwestern delicacies and family favorites on the table, and gifts for the children under a Christmas tree. The evening passed pleasantly, and before long it was time to venture into the cold for the ritual festivities at the Pueblo.

Moonlight bathed the Pueblo, illuminating its simple flowing lines and casting shadows in empty doorways. Everyone gathered in the square, some in native dress, others in jeans and boots, others like us wearing layer upon layer to ward off the chill. Jon hoisted Katie to his shoulders, and our daughter, Sophie, clambered up onto her dad's.

Everywhere, huge mounds of wood awaited the torch, and soon smoke burst forth above the crowd into the clear night sky. Sparks flew and flames roared, and the children cried to be put back on the ground where it felt safer. All around us, people whooped and hollered. A procession wound through the crowd behind a priest, who carried an elevated statue of the Virgin Mary dressed as a bride.

In the midst of these ancient religious rituals stood the little church, the Chapel of San Geronimo, its doors open to the stream of people passing down its aisles to the altar. Inside the chapel, in the blending of culture, belief, and ritual, we felt Dan's presence as the space around us filled with God's love and our longing. We bent our heads at the altar, and when we looked up, a glow from the outside fires lit the church, painting the walls inside and our faces with a vibrant orange wash. Illuminated, we three sisters held onto each other and walked tall back into the holy night.

BY DIANA THRIFT

Colors of Christmas

❦ ❦ ❦

THE CHRISTMAS SEASON always delights our vision with the rich tones of red, crimson, and scarlet—as well as silver and gold and everything that glitters. We think of this holiday as the brightest and boldest in hue.

Years ago, I learned that the color of Christmas is not in shades of red or green or silver or gold. Christmas is color-blind. It glitters from within and picks up the reflections from its surroundings. Who would have ever thought that a hospital ward could sparkle? But it did, and we were there to see it.

"Pete, Pete, can you hear me?" My grandmother practically woke the whole hospital ward as she called my grandfather back to consciousness. He was a construction worker, a simple man who used his hands to mix concrete, build girders, and lay stone. Even though his hands were like vises, he was not indestructible—as we had always thought. In fact, when he had his accident five days before Christmas, we discovered how human he really was.

We realized that Christmas was going to be very different that year. The absence of this quiet and warm man from our home would be excruciatingly obvious. So, since he could not be with us, we decided to bring Christmas to him. At the time, in the 1950s, hospitals did not cater to the average person. Perhaps the Rockefellers of the world had double rooms or even singles, but the construction workers were in wards—long wards with rows of beds, as many as 20 to a room, ten on each side.

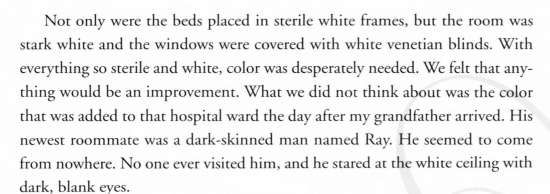

Not only were the beds placed in sterile white frames, but the room was stark white and the windows were covered with white venetian blinds. With everything so sterile and white, color was desperately needed. We felt that anything would be an improvement. What we did not think about was the color that was added to that hospital ward the day after my grandfather arrived. His newest roommate was a dark-skinned man named Ray. He seemed to come from nowhere. No one ever visited him, and he stared at the white ceiling with dark, blank eyes.

However, my grandmother had a way of making everyone, everywhere feel like part of her personal flock. After she was sure that my grandfather, her Pete, was awake, fully conscious and out of danger, she began to visit not only him but his ward neighbors. She brought garlands to drape on the bed frames and pine wreaths to place on the windowsills. She brought candles sprinkled with colored glitter. Daily, she carried in shopping bags full of homemade cookies and hot soup. We could not figure out how she kept it as hot as she did for the two-hour bus ride to the hospital until Gramps winked at us and glanced at his old thermos, which he had carried in his metal lunch pail.

Gram visited the hospital daily, and with each visit she learned a bit more about the dark-skinned loner in the next bed. What we noticed was that beside the fact that no one came to visit him, other visitors avoided him like he was not even there. Fortunately, Gram had her knack of breaking the ice. She did learn that Ray had no family in the area. His wife had died, and his children were young adults in another city, probably unable to visit during the holidays.

As a family, we worked to create a lovely holiday with not only the colors of Christmas but with the value of remembering the meaning. We talked at great

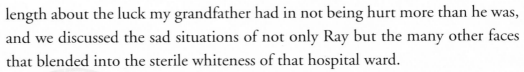

length about the luck my grandfather had in not being hurt more than he was, and we discussed the sad situations of not only Ray but the many other faces that blended into the sterile whiteness of that hospital ward.

Since Gramps and his ward neighbor could not be home with their families, Gram brought homemade dinner to them. We helped her haul in her freshly baked and sliced turkey, several trays of homemade pizza, chunks of cheese, a few loaves of bread, bottles of homemade red wine, and tins filled with Christmas cookies. She was talented beyond belief. And as odd a meal as it sounded, it was welcomed.

We not only enriched that ward with home-baked scents and the color of that ward with new shades of red and green, but we filled the space with sound. The ward echoed with laughter and talk and music. My uncle brought his accordion, and we sang our favorite Christmas carols. "O Come, All Ye Faithful" and "O Little Town of Bethlehem" took on a whole new dimension when accompanied by the squeezebox. My grandfather did not look as damaged as he did five days prior, and Ray proved that he had a deep, rich voice waiting to be heard.

We all knew that the Lord works in his own way and things happen in his time, not ours. However, that Christmas evening became a blessed event, as we visited and sang and ate together. Moreover, Ray's children appeared. They arrived after a long trip, the three of them, with simple gifts of love.

The Lord sent a miracle that day, and perhaps we do not need to know whether it was Grandma or Ray or his children. All we know is that it was a blessed day, with loving people celebrating the birth of Jesus.

By Elizabeth Toole

Decisions

❧   ❧   ❧

WHITE LIGHTS TWINKLING on Mom's Savannah holly blurred into halos through the guest bedroom window. As I sat in the rocker, the world seemed to stop as I contemplated what I had done. Dad slipped into the room, gave me a small, quick hug, and then left. My tears pooled again. Hugging was not something he usually did.

Separation papers were scheduled to be served on my husband this December afternoon. The boys and I were tucked away at my parents' house, where life always seemed to be comfortable and happy. "Jingle Bells" played from the doormat on the front porch. The logs in the fireplace crackled and snapped under homemade quilted stockings.

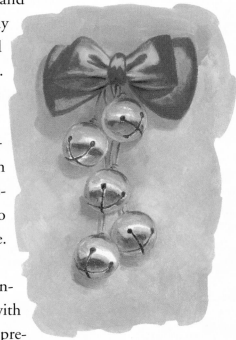

At 34, my reality train had jumped the track. I was the first-born, an honor student who had maintained high grades through college, married my high school sweetheart, and started a promising career. The house and promotions followed easily enough. Two children, born two years apart, and a dog completed the fairy tale. But our story didn't end "happily ever after."

Aching from sitting, crying, or just from living, I walked downstairs for coffee. Mom and the boys, ages five and seven, met me with an early present. To keep the boys upbeat and distracted, we all pretended we were "cheating" by opening the gift. The hand-decorated sweatshirt Mom made was revealed to oohs and ahs. How did she do it? How had she managed to create a 36-year marriage in Ozzie-and-Harriet style? I missed that gene somewhere along the way.

The little guys were fine—so far. But we were just starting this venture together, alone. Would they hate me years from now or respect my courage? They were my final deciding factor for doing this. But then again, they were why I wished I hadn't.

The holidays crept by and finally passed. I had to return to the scene of the domestic tragedy, our home. Everyday life continued. Returning to work felt like a charade. I smiled at co-workers, knowing they'd compare notes about how I looked or what I said. Day-care moms avoided the normal pleasantries. The house became a retreat, despite the For Sale sign in the yard.

Plummeting into self-pity, I managed to pull off the daily Murphy Brown routine until I reached home at night. With the boys in bed, I embraced *Wuthering Heights* in the bathtub, seemingly appropriate. When the boys went to visit their dad, I hugged a six-pack. Apparently lacking any tolerance for the stuff, I wound up clutching the toilet.

Feeling low one Saturday night, sitting at home with my eyes swollen from crying, I decided I'd go to church the next day. I hated the thought of all those eyes glancing away when I tried to meet their gaze, but it had been a few weeks since I'd been there and I thought it might be comforting to go.

When the minister began delivering his sermon, I was amazed to find that it was about divorce. "The Lord weeps to see his children in pain," he said soothingly. "His love is completely unconditional, as is any father's love for his child."

I knew of others who had divorced in the past, but I'd always felt distanced from them. Now, I was that person "someone else" knew. In spite of living my life "right," I had faltered and become "tainted." I felt shame as I remembered my own condescension toward those who had been divorced.

I sat in the back pew, absorbing every loving word the minister spoke. He seemed to be talking directly to me, saying I was a treasured child of God, capable of making flawed decisions and wrong turns. I was loved and could be loving to others, in spite of my human flaws. Even if I had made some bad choices, that didn't make me a bad person. I was an acceptable woman, worthy of being loved. Life was still good and well worth living.

Despite the adjustment of segregated parenting, my babies grew to be teenagers, who now tower over me. In contented amazement and continued hope, I watch as maturity dominates their actions and decisions. I've tried to teach them that life is a series of mistakes we all make and for which we are all held accountable. As the minister had said that day, "While we are not responsible for others' mistakes, we are responsible for acknowledging that others make them."

Christmas is still at my parents' house. The boys' stepdad and I stay in the same guest bedroom, with the cozy rocker and the twinkle lights glowing like halos outside the window. Now a little older and wiser, I rock and smile and feel accomplished. The sound of "Jingle Bells" playing from the front porch doormat swells a yearning within me—not for days gone by, but for a hopeful future for my sons and my husband . . . and for me.

BY HOPE CLARK

Holiday Cheer

AT CHRISTMAS PLAY and make good cheer
For Christmas comes but once a year.

THOMAS TUSSER (1524–1580)

The Kitty

❧ ❧ ❧

T HE RADIATOR HISSED. My pencil plowed a wood furrow in the scarred desktop, deepening an "x" carved by a previous child. Behind me, assorted midwinter sniffles and coughs punctuated Quiet Time.

Thumbing the pages of my fifth-grade reader, I stole a look around the classroom. My gaze lingered on the shopping bags squatting under the chairs of my two best friends. I didn't have to peek on the wire rack below my own to know a third sack waited there. I was uncomfortably aware; I couldn't ignore it if I wanted to. And, believe me, I wanted to.

The first day back to school was made more difficult by the January drab that trailed last month's glitter. Crayon drawings of carrot-nosed snowmen no longer danced down the corridor walls. No red and green balls bobbed from the ceiling; no "stained-glass" artwork gleamed in the windows; no jeweled trees winked from the bulletin boards. Even the spicy scent of clove-studded oranges had evaporated along with the decorations. There were no remnants to show that the holidays had come—and gone.

Yet the evidence lurked beneath my desk, and I dreaded the moment of reckoning. My heart beat in the same halting rhythm as the second hand on the big wall clock. Only seven minutes left until recess . . . and the unveiling.

During the weeks prior to Christmas, Pam, Gayle, and I had shared the same wish. Instead of sugarplums, we dreamed of The Kitty. The kitty with powder-puff white fur to rub against your cheek. The kitty with the unblinking topaz eyes that promised to keep secrets. The kitty whose tiny body was perfect for nestling in a young girl's hand. The little stuffed animal *everyone* craved that December of 1961.

The three of us plotted our strategy well. In the earliest days, in phase one of our plan, we did extra chores. We were cheerful and obliging. We dropped careful hints. We circled the kitty's description in the winter catalog, our insurance against paltry imitations. As Christmas drew nearer, we forged into phase two—reminding, bargaining, pleading, whining to our parents that everyone else would be getting one. Nothing was beneath us.

At my house, Mother was busy with the new baby. She handed Daddy her detailed list, pecked his cheek, and shooed him out the door. *This could be good,* I thought. As a shopper, Daddy was inexperienced but methodical. He would follow the list, no questions asked, and I already knew what was on it—because I had peeked (phase three). My kitty was a sure thing.

Following tradition, we opened presents one at a time

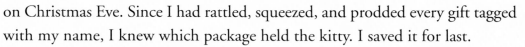

on Christmas Eve. Since I had rattled, squeezed, and prodded every gift tagged with my name, I knew which package held the kitty. I saved it for last.

The entire family watched. I guess they could feel my excitement. Shiny gold foil crinkled as my hands pressed the shape of it. Long pieces of tape curled as my nails peeled them back. A bit of soft white fur feathered the folded edge. Eyes closed, I slid my fingers inside to let them brush across a butter-soft nose, trace the length of tiny felt ears, and curl into luxurious fur. Smiling, I tugged away the wrappings and opened my eyes to . . . a skunk.

A stuffed *skunk*? It was a skunk, all right, complete with a long white stripe and beady black eyes and squatty little ears and . . .

I looked up—directly into Daddy's anxious grin—only half hearing his garbled explanation of lengthy store lines, empty shelves, and the exhaustive hunt for a suitable substitution. It felt like a giant snowball had settled in my stomach. I was a heartsick ten-year-old, torn between the crush of my own disappointment and the deep-rooted desire to keep the eager smile on my daddy's face.

"When I saw this, I couldn't believe my eyes," he gushed. *Me neither*, I thought.

"Just wait until the other kids see this," he said. *Can't wait.*

"Why, I'll bet you're the only girl in the whole school who got a skunk this Christmas," he nodded. "You'll be different." *No kidding*, I thought. *This really stinks.*

Even so, I swallowed back the tears clogging my throat, walked across the room to hug Daddy, and whispered a broken thank-you in his ear.

The harsh bell signaled recess.

Pam, Gayle, and I made our pilgrimage to the trunk of an ancient cotton-wood where we were shielded from the knife-edged wind. Like the Magi bearing gifts, we knelt beneath the tree. Pam opened her bag first. Reverently, she offered her palm-size kitten with the topaz eyes. "I call her Snowball."

Gayle was next. She cupped an identical ball of pristine white fluff. "I named mine Marshmallow."

By this time, all the other fifth-grade girls had encircled us, admiring and cooing. It was my turn. I swallowed and quickly blurted out, "I named mine . . . Stinky!"

Hesitating, I jerked back the rolled flap of the wrinkled brown sack, grabbed it by the bottom, and shook out the awful black skunk. In a silence that seemed to last forever, I glanced up. Wide-eyed girls stared at Stinky. A scattered few giggled, and they all started to chatter at once.

"A skunk! He's so cute!"

"Can I see him?"

"He's made out of genuine rabbit fur!"

"Pass him over here. Oh look, you can make his tail bend."

"I wish I'd gotten one of these."

Flushing as bright as Rudolph's nose, I combed my fingers through the onyx fur. Girls pressed nearer, huddled against the cold, to ask questions and beg for chances to hold the unparalleled pet. Pam turned to Gayle.

"Why, I bet she's the only girl in the whole school who got a skunk for Christmas!"

My grin stretched from ear to ear. *Thanks to Daddy,* I thought.

BY CAROL McADOO REHME

Reindeer Hooves

"MOMMY, MOMMY! Do you think they left the North Pole yet?" my four-year-old son anxiously queried in an unusually deep voice.

"Gosh, I don't know, Kev," I replied. But then, after thinking about the anticipation in his eyes and voice, I corrected myself and said decidedly, "Oh yes, absolutely, positively, yes. Santa and the reindeer have definitely left the North Pole by now."

This little imp of a child grinned from ear to ear and began describing what the reindeer were discussing on their flight through the sky as they visited every child in the world. Rudolph, of course, was the brightest because he was smart enough to turn his nose on and off like a blinking red light. He would tell them what the weather was, which country they would visit first, what the dangers were of landing on a weak roof, and to listen only to Santa for their directions. He reminded me that "even the reindeers are not allowed to talk to strangers," as if there would be a lot of them racing around the sky. . . .

Kevin began to sift through Christmas cookies to find the most perfect cookies to leave for Santa. After much debate, he decided that "this reindeer with the chocolate horns looks like the one Santa would want. So does this angel with yellow sprinkles and this toy soldier with a big red hat and this star like the one who saw Jesus. . . ."

He gently put them onto the dish he made in nursery school, licking his fingers after each placement and picking off a chocolate jimmy or two. Kev poured Santa a glass of milk, placed it next to the cookies on the dish, and toddled to bed as he wondered when they would arrive.

"Do you think Santa will knock or come down the chimney? Will he burn his tummy, or does he have on fireproof underwear? Can the reindeer come in, too?" Finally, the little guy with the twinkling brown eyes and mop of chestnut hair could not think of any more things to say, and he fell asleep . . . until . . .

Around midnight, Kevin shrieked, "I hear them, I hear them! They're on the roof! Santa's reindeers are on the roof!" He barreled down the stairs, and as he tornadoed through the kitchen he stopped on a dime, practically falling on the cookie dish. His eyes looked as though they would pop out of his head as he breathlessly sang, "Santa ate all the cookies! Santa ate all the cookies! Look, Mommy, they're gone and the milk is gone and look, the crumbs are everywhere! I bet he fed the reindeers, too!" Kevin never did convince his brother and sister that he had heard reindeer hooves on the roof. But he believed it . . . for years and years and years. . . .

BY ELIZABETH TOOLE

The Pin

❦ ❦ ❦

WHEN I WAS YOUNG, the general store wove a powerful spell over me. Upon those dusty, crammed shelves sat pleasure, temptation, and once, for me, a heart's desire.

A glass-enclosed candy display case presented the main attraction for kids. Beyond that finger-smudged barrier lay a confectionery wonderland. I lingered over my favorites, choosing from caramel pinwheels, lemon drops, and chocolate kisses and passing over peppermint sticks, licorice strings, and root beer barrels. All transactions were contemplated deeply. One for a penny or two for a penny depended upon whether I was shopping for only myself or if I was sharing.

Summertime brought miniature wax soda bottles filled with a swallow of sweet liquid and tiny candy ice cream cones topped with sugar-sprinkled marshmallow. I enjoyed these all summer long, then licked my lips as Halloween approached and candy corn and wax teeth took their place.

I was eight, and, on a casual browse through the merchandise room, I saw something that stopped me in my tracks. Fastened to a small square of white cardboard, high up on a shelf where nothing could happen to it, sat the most beautiful piece of jewelry I had ever seen. I stood transfixed as my friends moved on, and I studied the details of the pink-and-white rhinestone flower upon a golden stem. Though not exactly the pearl of great price, to a third-

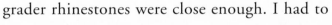

grader rhinestones were close enough. I had to have it. At the time, I had never heard of layaway or buying on credit. I just started saving my money.

I accompanied my friends to the store and visited my pin while they conducted business over the penny candy. No gumdrops for me; no butterscotch, either. Every penny I had was carefully socked away in my piggy bank and taken out every night to be counted. The price of the piece of jewelry amounted to less than a dollar, but when measured in chocolate drops and coconut strips, it seemed impressive.

Red-and-white-striped candy canes and chocolate Santas had replaced Halloween fare when I finally exchanged my pennies, nickels, and dimes for the pin I coveted. The proprietor smiled as I carefully counted out my change. If she had noticed my daily pilgrimages to the jewelry counter, she never said, but her smile, as she wrapped the pin in tissue and handed it over, was tender.

I was once again free to indulge my sweet tooth to my heart's content. I had discovered, however, something sweeter than all the candy I had sacrificed. On Christmas there would be a special package under our tree. Inside would be the prettiest pin I had ever seen, and the tag would say, "For my mom."

By Glenda Emigh

A Rock 'n' Roll Christmas

❧   ❧   ❧

PLUMP SNOWFLAKES FELL early in the winter of 1956, and I focused my imagination on Christmas. I could hardly wait. I was 13 and felt that this year I deserved a more grown-up gift than the customary baby doll. I'd talked to Mama about it months before, and she had agreed with me. We children, two boys and four girls, knew not to ask for extras, but Christmas was always different. The possibilities were endless, and this year I knew exactly what I wanted.

In September of that year, I fell in love. Madly, passionately, by the purest sense of any teenage girl's imagination, in love. I sat cross-legged on my parents' living room floor, mesmerized by the television—specifically, the *Ed Sullivan Show*. I looked at the TV screen and into the face of Elvis Presley. That winter night, I lost my heart to Elvis and rock 'n' roll, in that order. I thought between the two, I'd found my heaven and earth.

Our only source of music was a small Philco radio above the kitchen sink; the dial was set to a country music station. Being the oldest girl of six children in the 1950s, my chores were plentiful and centered mainly in the kitchen. With good grades and hard work to support me, I begged Mama to let me listen to the new rock 'n' roll station, at least while I washed the dinner dishes at night.

I listened carefully to the lyrics of every song, and soon I knew every word. A cooking utensil became my microphone, while I sang and danced in my ankle socks and saddle shoes to the tunes rocking from the little radio. Nothing else made me happier, despite the soapsuds running down my arms, dripping onto the cracked linoleum floor.

I believed I sang as well as the recording artists I listened to each night. It became such an obsession for me, I actually looked forward to doing the dishes so I could be alone to sing my songs. In rolled-up jeans and a sweater set from my grandparents, I rehearsed my act to perfection. The door separating the kitchen from the rest of the house assured me an isolated stage. As you can imagine, it took a long time for me to get the dishes done.

One night, while my hips swayed to an Elvis tune, I overheard Mama and Dad discussing finances at the dining room table. It didn't sound very good. I knew my dad was out of work, but Mama had taken a job at Sears, Roebuck. So I thought we were doing all right. I tiptoed to the door that divided my world from the rest of the house and listened. They were discussing how little money was left over from the bills to spend on Christmas. My heart went out to them, and a knot formed in my throat. They sounded so sad.

Before I could think of the repercussions, I swung the door open and went to stand by my mother.

"I just want you both to know," I blurted, "that I'm not a child anymore, and I don't really need Christmas presents. Take the money you planned to spend on me and buy presents for the little kids instead."

Mama's arm encircled my waist, and she looked up into my face. She looked so tired. Then she surprised me. She laid her head against me and started to sob.

What went wrong? I thought this would be a relief.

"No, no," Daddy said, shaking his head, rubbing his wet eyes beneath his glasses. "We'll work something out. Go finish the dishes, angel."

I understood then that I had embarrassed them. Money, in any form or lack thereof, was never discussed in front of the children. I took the dismissal with a heavy heart and sadly returned to the kitchen. I didn't play the radio anymore that night because the Christmas songs made me cry. I was a fool to tell them to forget about a present for me. Why did I do that? Why didn't I just keep my mouth shut? When I turned back to my chores, I found the suds gone and the dishwater cold, just like my dreams. Pulling the plug, I saw the chance of having my very own record player disappear.

Christmas Eve arrived, and all the younger kids went to bed early. Mama was full of Christmas spirit, humming old hymns as she wrapped each gift, making pretty bows with a flourish. As always, I assisted Mama with wrapping the presents and writing out gift tags, a job I usually enjoyed, but I was upset that she couldn't see how sad I had become. Why was she making me help when there was no gift for me?

Surveying the table, I saw a doll for each of the girls and some trucks for little Stevie. My older brother would receive a new pair of jeans and a plaid flannel shirt to keep him warm. Soon all the presents were wrapped and ready, but there was not a thing for me. With our task completed, Mama thanked me and shooed me off to bed.

Christmas dawned cold and windy with a snowstorm that masked the view from my window. Three giggling little sisters climbed into my bed, begging me to see if Santa had come during the night. Nudging them off the bed, I took my sisters to the next room and woke our brothers. I told them all to put on robes and slippers as I did the same. Leading them to the main hallway, I instructed them to wait while I woke Mama and Daddy. Soon everyone was up and ready, and we entered the living room.

The tree, decorated with angels and lighted bubble candles, dominated the bay windows, and the heavy snowfall in the background created a magnificent scene. Too bad we had such a pretty tree with nothing under it for me!

Daddy handed out stockings filled with the requisite gifts: an apple or orange, peppermints or chocolate, coloring books or cut-out paper dolls—all special treats welcomed with oohs and aahs. Finally, Daddy progressed to the tree and passed out the precious gifts one by one. Cries of glee erupted from around the room, and soon there was nothing left beneath the tree but an old, tinsel-strewn tree skirt.

Tears of self-pity pricked my eyes, but I was deter-mined not to let anyone see me cry. I took a deep breath and joined the kids, who were still unwrap-ping puzzles, games, and books. Through my heartache, I suddenly heard music. I shushed the kids and concentrated on the lyrics. The song I heard was "My Special Angel." I smiled since Daddy always called me his angel. Through blurry eyes I looked at him, sitting in his favorite chair, and I detected a twitch of a grin. Mama's eyes twinkled mischievously.

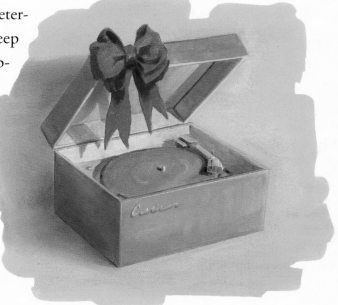

"What's going on?" I asked, looking from one to the other. "Where is that music coming from?"

Daddy tried to be serious: "I don't know what you're talking about. I don't hear any music."

I scrambled from the floor and took a step toward his chair. The closer I got, the louder the music was. I circled the old chair and found a beautiful record player with a big red bow and my name on the tag. Through my tears, I gave Daddy a big hug, then ran to Mama and kissed her, too. The song ended, and Daddy showed me how the player worked, starting the record over again. He explained that they had only enough money to buy one record, but he promised they would buy me more. I didn't care—it was mine! My parents had not forgotten me.

Although I cherished that beloved record player, that was not what lifted my heart and made that Christmas so special. Rather, it was the music in my parents' hearts that made my spirit dance.

By Judith Givens

The holly's up,
the house is all bright,
The tree is ready,
The candles alight;
Rejoice and be glad,
all children tonight!
Carl August Peter Cornelius
Der Christbaum

A Tale of Two Christmas Cakes

🍃 🍃 🍃

*E*VERY YEAR, AS THE holidays approach, I get out my recipes for two special Christmas cakes, one a rich Southern pecan cake, the other a spicy Old World honey cake. These cakes are from family recipes, from great-grandmothers and *babcias,* from kitchens as far apart as Knoxville, Tennessee, and Warsaw, Poland. These cakes bake long and slow and fill the air with an exotic bouquet. Breathing them in reminds me that I am a link with the women who made the cakes before me and the ones who will make them in the future.

The recipe for the first cake harkens back to my great-grandmother, Serena Caroline Bellamy. It has passed through four generations of Southern women who loved pecans as much as I do. Nowadays, the very mention of Granny's pecan cake brings sighs to my parents and sisters, who remember those wonderful cakes and hope that maybe this year I'll make it just like Granny used to.

I remember Christmases when I was a child, when that special box came all the way from Tennessee. I remember the look on my mother's face—reverence, almost—as she lifted out the big tin, opened it, and proudly displayed what was inside: a beautiful golden-brown cake, topped with whole pecans and cherries and wrapped in thin, purple, wine-soaked cloth.

My mother never made the cake, but she saved the family recipe, and when I became a young mother myself, I asked for it. It was a difficult recipe, one

that measured ingredients by weight instead of volume. It called for pans lined with brown paper, and the cake needed to be baked for four hours in a 250-degree oven.

The first time I made it, I didn't notice those last two critical details until I finished stirring in the pecans at 10 P.M.—and realized that my apartment oven couldn't even warm up below 350. I set the alarm and got up at 2 A.M. to take it out. It was dry, and it fell apart when I cut it, but it tasted wonderful.

The next year I converted those measurements from pounds to cups. I also considered fortifying myself with a small glass of the port wine that flavors this cake. The wine mingles its delicate flavor with the rich, dark nectar of molasses and the tingle of cinnamon and nutmeg.

It's 25 years later, and I still make the cake nearly every year. I love seeing my daughters' eyes grow big as the combination of grape juice, wine, and molasses turns the batter a most unusual color—sort of a plum-kissed brown.

Although the cake always ends up delicious, it somehow never comes out quite as perfectly as my grandmother's. But that's okay, because the cake, to me, is much more than just a cake: It's a tradition, a tradition I'm proud to have preserved, something special that brings a bit of our family history to life and honors those women who made the cake.

My daughters, who are half Polish, will perhaps be more inclined to make the other Christmas cake, the one from their Polish grandmother, or *babcia*, Jadwiga Olszeneczka Krajewski. This cake, a dark, spicy honey cake called *piernik*, is my husband's all-time favorite—and not only at Christmas.

In their family, any special occasion calls for *piernik*. Of course, his mother's *pierniks* were always wonderful, even when she had to use artificial honey

because real honey was scarce in Poland. And if she ever makes one that's less than perfect, it is easily excused. "It's a temperamental cake," shrugs my father-in-law, "especially when you use real honey."

Perhaps that's why my *pierniks*—made with real honey—were always a disaster, sagging inexplicably into a gooey, aromatic mess. This, despite our careful conversions of European kilograms and decagrams into standard U.S. cups and teaspoons. But some ingredients, like flour and leavening agents, are not the same in Europe as they are here. Could that have been the problem? It didn't matter. After years of near misses and disasters with this cake, I swore I'd never make it again.

After a while, of course, I agreed to try it one last time. I searched through cookbooks—both Polish and American—looking for a similar recipe or, lacking that, a clue. What I noticed was that most recipes, especially the few using honey, called for baking powder, not baking soda, as mine did. When I substituted double-acting baking powder for the soda—*voila!*—a marvelous *piernik* at last.

These cakes have taught me a lot—not so much about baking as about the value of preserving even little bits of our heritage to pass along to our children and grandchildren. The future is never certain. But I at least feel fairly certain that wherever they are, come November, my daughters will begin to get that urge to get out the family recipes for pecan cake and *piernik,* to try those special holiday cakes that their mother, grandmother, and great-great-grandmother made before them. And one day, like me, they're bound to stand in their kitchens and reflect on the priceless traditions that we hand down within our families.

BY DIANA THRIFT

Midnight Mass

WHEN CINDY AND HER TWO young children visited her out-of-state parents on Christmas weekend, they made sure to arrive early enough for Christmas Eve mass. After all, it was a family tradition.

Christmas Eve was picture-postcard perfect, crisp and cold. Three generations walked hand-in-hand down the sidewalk while a fresh snow muffled their footsteps and blanketed the streets. Their breath puffed out in small clouds, and trees cast lacy night shadows beneath the street lamps.

Inside the hushed cathedral, the piney scent of evergreens was warmed by dozens of candles. Even though she had converted to another religion a few years ago, Cindy found herself slipping easily into the ritual and ceremony of midnight mass. It was comfortable. Even welcoming.

What an excellent opportunity this was, she decided, to expose her young children to their legacy. They were witnessing and experiencing the formalities and heritage of their grandparents' faith. And it could only enhance the true meaning of Christmas, spiritual lessons she had worked diligently to teach them this December.

She particularly enjoyed watching wide-eyed Scott. Far from being sleepy at that late hour, her four-year-old son sat poised and alert. Cindy was amazed. Scott didn't wiggle; he didn't fidget; he didn't even whisper. Instead, Scott observed the songs and chants. He mimicked the kneeling. He concentrated on each ritual of the service with an intense and reverent silence particularly foreign to his usually exuberant nature.

Cindy gauged each of his reactions. She was certain Scott was remembering the Christmas story she had read to him each night that month. Certain he was full of the wonder of the season. Certain he was awed by the solemnity of the occasion.

Immediately outside the church, he slipped his mittened hand into his grandpa's.

"How did you like the service, Scott?" Grandpa asked. Cindy leaned closer, awaiting the answer. Which of her lessons had Scott related to? Faith? Gratitude? Giving? She could hardly wait to hear what made the biggest impression.

"Fine." Scott swung around and looked up. "But Grandpa, why did you have to walk in that long line to the front?"

"Why, Scott, I went to the priest to receive communion. Don't your parents take the sacrament when you go to church?"

"Well, yes," he replied. Scott thought a long minute, then pompously invited, "But next time, Grandpa, I've decided you should come with us. At our church, they deliver!"

BY CAROL McADOO REHME

Reindeer on the Roof

❧ ❧ ❧

JUSTIN GALLOPED INTO the kitchen, where his mother and aunt were cutting out Christmas cookies. "Guess what, Mom!" he said. "There isn't really a Santa Claus!"

"Oh, is that right? What makes you think so?" Sandy asked.

"I was playing in Grandpa's basement this morning, and I found a Santa suit. I always *thought* Santa was really Grandpa, but now I know for sure." He snagged an iced reindeer cookie and bit into it with gusto.

"Okay, big guy, I guess you know the truth," Sandy said with a smile. "But don't tell Grandpa yet. He isn't ready to stop pretending." She glanced at Tammy, and the two sisters burst out laughing.

"What's so funny?" Justin asked.

"We were just remembering when we were kids," his mom replied. "When I was seven and Aunt Tammy was five, we decided that there wasn't a Santa, and we started arguing about it with your grandpa. So he thought of a plan to convince us."

"What did he do?"

"After we were in bed on Christmas Eve, Grandpa climbed onto the roof of our house with some old sleigh bells. His plan was to stomp around the roof like reindeer and ring those bells. He was going to shout 'Ho, ho, ho!' down the chimney."

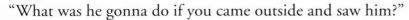

"What was he gonna do if you came outside and saw him?"

"Well, his plan was to climb down. The ladder was at the back of the house, and Grandma was supposed to take us out the front. We would look up at the roof and Grandma would say, 'I guess Santa just flew away.'"

"Is that what happened?"

"Not exactly. Grandpa is afraid of heights. Once he was up there, he felt so woozy that he accidentally kicked the ladder, and it fell to the ground. There he was—stranded high up on the roof with no way to get off."

"What did he do?"

"Instead of 'Ho, ho, ho!,' we heard 'Help, help, help!'"

"When he yelled," Aunt Tammy continued, "our dog started barking. That made the other dogs in the neighborhood bark, too. Pretty soon the neighbors came out to see what was wrong. Someone called the police and the fire department. The local TV station even sent a reporter and camera crew."

"Did the firemen get him down?"

"They tried, but he was holding on to the chimney very tightly. Finally, Grandpa's friend, Mr. Donnelly, did it. He owned a truck with a cherry picker—you know, one of those big buckets people stand in when they have to work up high—and he persuaded Grandpa to get into it."

"Wish I was there to see Grandpa in the cherry picker," Justin giggled. "I guess I better pretend I believe in Santa for a while longer. When do you think I can stop?"

His aunt smiled. "When there's another little boy or girl in the family who thinks Santa's real," she said.

BY SANDY KOEHLER WRIGHT AND TAMMY WRIGHT, AS TOLD TO ANN RUSSELL

The Ghost of Christmas Trees Past

A FEW WEEKS BEFORE Christmas one year, my husband and I visited a quaint town in the north Georgia mountains. At a country Christmas store, I found exactly what I wanted—a large artificial tree adorned with mauve ornaments, ribbons, and lace. The tree towered over all the others and was—in a word—majestic.

Staring at it, I knew I must have that tree. I deserved it! After all those years of plain-Jane Christmas trees, I would have the best. This glorious designer tree would look spectacular in its place of honor in front of the bay window. The neighbors would gasp in astonishment and envy when they saw my beautiful tree. Surely my grown children would be glad to leave all those old handmade ornaments in the basement. I certainly wouldn't miss dragging out that 15-year-old torn and flattened construction paper chain or the clothespin reindeer with its missing left eye. Gone would be the tinfoil bell and my son's metal star.

Picturing these ornaments, I smiled. Though it's been years now, I can still see Nathan's dad holding a nail while Nathan patiently hammered his name across a cut-out star. "Mama, look!" he shouted when he finished. His eyes shone bright as he handed me his treasure.

And that clothespin reindeer! My daughter had almost exploded with joy as she explained, step by step, how she created the little reindeer for me at school. Another time, she had made a Christmas bell ornament from a miniature flowerpot she had decorated with green and red rickrack.

One year, both of my kids and I sat for hours cutting Christmas stockings out of felt. Those stockings, featuring my children's names boldly—if a little sloppily—in glitter, were somewhere in that box of time-worn and faded ornaments. I recalled a plaster mold of Nathan's hands—with his name and age (five) scrawled on the back—that I always hung in a place of honor on the front of the tree.

I looked again at the stately tree adorned in mauve ornaments and lace. Suddenly, it began to lose its luster. It looked very nice there in that store, but that's where it would stay.

Christmas brought my adult children home that year. Laughter filled the family room as we decorated the sweet-smelling cedar Christmas tree we had chopped down just that afternoon—the whole family together on an adventure reminiscent of those we had gone on for all previous Christmases. "Look, Mom," my daughter said, beaming at me. She giggled as she hung the plaster mold in its usual place of honor.

I looked at our tree with satisfaction, knowing that no more beautiful Christmas tree had ever existed.

BY NANETTE THORNTON SNIPES

Finding the Perfect Gift

❧   ❧   ❧

WHEN IT COMES TO SHOPPING, just call me Mr. Doofus, especially during the Christmas season.

Shopping has never been high on my list of things to do. Malls intimidate me to the point of paralysis. Even the word suggests what might happen to me if I am not careful. Regardless of which mall I'm in, I always find myself wandering around with a glazed look in my eyes, mumbling incoherently.

Some people, such as my wife, have mastered the art of shopping at the mall. I tip my hat reverently to these people. Unlike me, they have faced the ugly Mall Monster and not only defeated him but made him their servant.

I honestly never know what to buy people at Christmastime. When I do purchase a gift, I begin to panic, worrying that the person will not like it or that it will not fit. I cannot tell you how many times, after buying a gift, I have in trepidation returned it for a refund. One year I bought the same gift three times before the salesperson refused to wait on me anymore.

This past week, though, I braced myself, made sure my life insurance and will were up to date, and ventured to the mall to do some Christmas shopping. My mission was to purchase a Christmas gift for my wife.

I have known this lady for more than 25 years, and I still have trouble knowing what to get her for Christmas. Once I gave her a lovely wristwatch, and she seemed pleased with my choice. So I gave her another one—for four

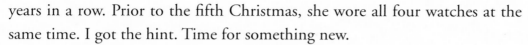

years in a row. Prior to the fifth Christmas, she wore all four watches at the same time. I got the hint. Time for something new.

I arrived at the mall early. Admittedly I was a little nervous, so I treated myself to a cup of coffee and a donut. After all, this was a special occasion, and I was not going to spare anything in my quest.

Not knowing how to properly conduct myself, I decided to sit on a bench and watch the shoppers. Soon it was lunchtime, and I was ravenous. This kind of work really makes a person hungry. Around 3 P.M., I finally was able to settle down to the task at hand. I soon found myself wandering in and out of shop after shop, not really focusing on anything I thought would suit my wife. Every shop began looking like the last shop until the circular mall seemed to spin around, with noise and music and glitz, like a swirling ride at a fiendish amusement park.

When I finally came to my senses, I quickly escaped to safety, bolting out of the mall as if the hounds of hell were nipping at my heels.

Safe in my office, I wondered if God had the same problem when it came to giving gifts. What could God really give? Then it dawned on me. "For God so loved the world, that he gave his only begotten Son, that whosoever believeth in him should not perish, but have everlasting life" (John 3:16, KJV).

Yes, God had given us the greatest gift of all, the perfect gift—Jesus Christ. It is, of course, the reason we celebrate this joyous holiday.

Now inspired, I continued the search for my wife's ideal present. I ventured into cyberspace—the World Wide Web!

Don't ask me how I fared. . . .

BY REV. JAMES L. SNYDER

Teensy-Weensy

❧ ❧ ❧

"THANK YOU," I TOLD the mail carrier, after signing for the small package. I shook the package. It gave a satisfying rattle.

I knew what it contained, and my gloom immediately began to lift. Holidays are difficult when you live alone, as I was finding out. It had been six months since my Arnold had passed, but leave it to a sister to brighten even loss's darkest corners. Carrie has been doing that as long as I can remember.

It had been a dark November a half-century ago. Coal dust covered our town, just as fear did our lives.

In the early '50s, our southern town lived under the shadow of "The Bomb." We were close to Oak Ridge, Tennessee, a strategic location, and this was predicted to be *the* year when bombs might fall. At school, where I was in third grade and Carrie in fifth, fire drills were replaced with air-raid drills. Carrie and I had already conceived a brave plan to escape and go home. Our family would stick together, we vowed, even concocting a plan to get our father home from work so he could hide in the basement with the two of us, as well as five-year-old Judith, our baby brother Sean, and Mother.

How big a celebration can you plan to ring in the holidays under such a threatening cloud?

Since Halloween, our family had worried but found no easy answer. Finally, our parents opted for streamlining our holidays in case we had to make a quick

evacuation. It took Carrie about a minute to translate the word "streamlined" into "no Christmas tree."

No tree? Unthinkable.

Not to worry, Carrie said.

Smiling in triumph, she unveiled her secret that night at supper. It was the smallest tree I had ever seen: a small, gold lapel pin in the shape of a Christmas tree. We children took turns wearing it right next to our hearts when it wasn't propped in a flowerpot on a nest of fake snow. True, its surroundings dwarfed it, but as Carrie pointed out, when you squinted, it looked larger.

Carrie's determination was contagious. In a moment of high-spirited defiance, Mother ordered a turkey from the poultry man, and Father resumed his hammering in the garage that doubled as his workshop.

Christmas morning arrived in a flurry of snowy grace. There was, at least for the moment, peace on earth. Our presents surrounded the splendid tiny tree in its flowerpot nest, "shining far brighter than anything that small had any right to do," as my Mother said in bemusement. Carrie's funny little tree changed what could have been a bleak holiday into one that continues to dazzle even in memory.

Over the years, Carrie has sent the pin (with a strict admonishment to return it to her promptly after the holidays) to any family member who needs some extra holiday spirit. Each time, spirits lift, bruised feelings brush themselves off, and hope brings possibilities into life-size proportion.

It's going to be a wonderful Christmas after all.

BY MARGARET ANNE HUFFMAN

Where's Daddy?

❦ ❦ ❦

Christmas Eve was a joyous occasion in our home, as usual. We had our traditional meal, sharing it with our practically grown children, my parents, my husband's mother, and a handful of friends.

Midway through dinner, my 19-year-old daughter, Anne, mentioned that it was getting late. "Santa is usually here by now. Do you think his sleigh got stuck on the thruway?" We all laughed, but she continued: "Santa is always here by now. It's almost nine o'clock." It was as though she was getting panicky over the jolly old soul not getting here.

Her father chimed in. "I am so tired of always missing Santa. I'm not going anywhere tonight, just in case he gets here late."

Again we all laughed. Our second son, Edward, rolled his eyes. "Dad, we knew it was you all those years," he said. "We could tell. You either forgot to change your shoes or your hair peeped through.

"Oh, come on," their father remarked indignantly. "I am your father and Santa is Santa. And to prove that to you, I am *not* leaving the couch tonight."

Edward reminded us of the year Santa rang the doorbell. "Like Santa has to ring the doorbell," he said. Then Edward teased Anne about the time Santa visited and she was frightened half to death. "Your eyes got as big as light bulbs and practically bugged out of your head when he walked through the door. You went screaming across the room to Mom."

"You know, just one of these years I would love to see this guy up close and personal," their dad yawned.

"I guess I can take the blame for Dad always missing Santa," I explained. "No matter how much I shop for the holidays, and how many lists I make, I always seem to forget something I really need. As you little angels were growing up, it was always easier for Daddy to run to the store in the evening."

"Sure, Ma," Jimmy assured me. "It was easier because he made the fastest quick-change in the world. After all those years of practice, he had his Santa transformation down to a science. Remember the year he forgot to take off his wedding ring? Or does Santa have one exactly like Dad's?"

I responded by beginning to clear away the dishes; the children were a huge help as always. The routine was moving along quickly, and we became engrossed in our usual holiday banter. Suddenly, the chaos was interrupted by a bellowing "Ho! Ho! Ho!" erupting from the front of the house.

And what did our wondrous eyes behold, once again, as in every year previous? Santa had arrived! And amazingly, he did *not* ring the doorbell or knock. He simply walked in.

He practically ran up to Anne, scooped her off her feet, and reminded her of years ago with, "Ho, ho, ho, Annie! You are not going to run away screaming tonight, are you?" He reached in his bag and pulled out a golf ball and reminded her to practice if she wanted to do well in the springtime. "The captain of the golf team has to practice!"

He danced around everyone who was there. The camera flashed at each person as he visited with them. Santa hugged my mother-in-law, and she just beamed. You would have thought she was embracing her own child!

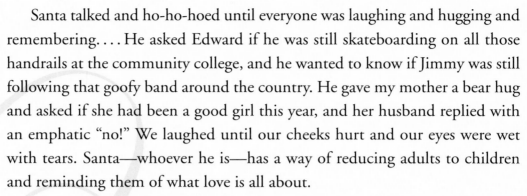

Santa talked and ho-ho-hoed until everyone was laughing and hugging and remembering. . . . He asked Edward if he was still skateboarding on all those handrails at the community college, and he wanted to know if Jimmy was still following that goofy band around the country. He gave my mother a bear hug and asked if she had been a good girl this year, and her husband replied with an emphatic "no!" We laughed until our cheeks hurt and our eyes were wet with tears. Santa—whoever he is—has a way of reducing adults to children and reminding them of what love is all about.

Santa passed out his gifts and announced, "Well, boys and girls, I have to get going because I have a billion other houses to visit—literally." We all gave him one last hug, and out the door he went.

When the ruckus calmed down, Anne asked, "Where's Daddy?" And we all giggled as we always do. "So where do you think he was this time?"

My husband strolled in from the kitchen, as he always had, very nonchalantly reaching for "just one more cookie, and that will be it for me tonight!" Jimmy questioned him: "Dad, where were you? You missed Santa again."

His father stared at him with a look of horror and disappointment. "You have got to be kidding me. Not again! I had to get gas before we went to church. My tank was just about on empty." He shook his head as he munched on the remainder of another cookie and sadly pouted, "I guess I will never see Santa. He never comes when I am here."

I simply smiled, grabbed my husband's hand, and said, "Too bad you missed him again. I gave him a hug for you!" Then I wiped the cookie crumbs from his chin and whispered, "Thanks for the memories."

BY ELIZABETH TOOLE